Lieutenant James Downing didn't just survive Pearl Harbor—he fought there. On the deck of his battleship, with Japanese planes raining down, he faced the flames of a man-made hell. And now he takes us back, to the day when evil failed to destroy faith and to the birth of a new American spirit, one that reigns to this day. *The Other Side of Infamy* is a priceless story by the rarest of authors: a battleship man at Pearl Harbor. There is no higher title.

ADAM MAKOS
New York Times bestselling author of *A Higher Call*

Jim Downing's story of courage, resilience, and faith is a must-read. He was already an original member of The Navigators ministry when he was caught up in the middle of the attack on Pearl Harbor. Jim ran into danger knowing his eternal destiny was secure—and his whole life has been devoted to sharing that hope with others.

JIM DALY
President of Focus on the Family

Jim Downing's memoir of his war years is both heart stirring and motivational. I read the book in two days, putting aside everything else I could.

GARY COOMBS
Shadow Mountain Community Church

The Other Side of Infamy is the compelling and beautiful story of an ordinary man experiencing extraordinary, world-changing events while abiding in Christ, meditating on his Word, and following Jesus in everything. It has been my great privilege to count Jim Downing as my friend and mentor for several decades. I can assure you that this remarkable story is not mere fiction.

ROBBY BUTLER
Editor of *Stubborn Perseverance*

THE OTHER SIDE OF INFAMY

MY JOURNEY THROUGH PEARL HARBOR
AND THE WORLD OF WAR

JIM DOWNING

WITH JAMES LUND

A NavPress resource published in alliance
with Tyndale House Publishers, Inc.

NavPress is the publishing ministry of The Navigators, an international Christian organization and leader in personal spiritual development. NavPress is committed to helping people grow spiritually and enjoy lives of meaning and hope through personal and group resources that are biblically rooted, culturally relevant, and highly practical.

For more information, visit www.NavPress.com.

The Other Side of Infamy: My Journey through Pearl Harbor and the World of War

Copyright © 2016 by James Downing. All rights reserved.

A NavPress resource published in alliance with Tyndale House Publishers, Inc.

NAVPRESS and the NAVPRESS logo are registered trademarks of NavPress, The Navigators, Colorado Springs, CO. *TYNDALE* is a registered trademark of Tyndale House Publishers, Inc. Absence of ® in connection with marks of NavPress or other parties does not indicate an absence of registration of those marks.

The Team:
Don Pape, Publisher
David Zimmerman, Acquiring Editor
Daniel Farrell, Designer

Cover, insert page 5 top, page 6, and back cover top left photographs are from the National Archives, public domain.

Photographs on insert page 5 bottom and back cover top right are courtesy of The Navigators and are used with permission.

Back cover photograph of damaged photograph copyright © Shikhar Bhattarai/iStockphoto. All rights reserved.

All other photographs are from the personal collection of the author and are used with permission. Some photographs were taken by US Navy personnel.

Scripture quotations are taken from the *Holy Bible*, King James Version.

Some of the anecdotal illustrations in this book are true to life and are included with the permission of the persons involved. All other illustrations are composites of real situations, and any resemblance to people living or dead is purely coincidental.

For information about special discounts for bulk purchases, please contact Tyndale House Publishers at csresponse@tyndale.com, or call 1-800-323-9400.

Cataloging-in-Publication Data is available.

ISBN 978-1-63146-744-8 (hardback)
ISBN 978-1-63146-627-4 (softcover)

Printed in the United States of America

23 22 21 20 19 18 17
12 11 10   9   8   7

CONTENTS

Prologue *vii*

1. Dreams and Shadows *1*
2. The Real World *17*
3. Sweet Music *35*
4. Inside Man *49*
5. Then There Was Morena *63*
6. Fury on Oahu *75*
7. A Different World *93*
8. No Sacrifice Too Great *107*
9. The Buck Stops Here *121*
10. From Hot to Cold *135*
11. Captain Downing *149*
12. Castle Bravo *161*
13. Endings and Beginnings *177*

Epilogue *187*
Appendix: Honoring Jim Downing—
    Congressional Record *191*
Notes *195*
About the Authors *199*

PROLOGUE

SOFT LIGHT REFLECTED by a nearly full moon bathes a peaceful Pacific island in a blanket of white. Azure ocean waves lap gently at still-warm sandy beaches. Koa trees in lush rain forests stretch for the sky while hibiscus flowers in verdant gardens wait for their next opportunity to bloom.

It is another enchanting Saturday night on the tropical paradise called Oahu, and most of the thousands of American servicemen and -women stationed here are ready to give in to its charms. Some who are advanced in rank enjoy a dance at an officers' club. Many enlisted men partake of the pleasures offered in downtown Honolulu: taverns and shops with names such as Two Jacks, the Mint, and the New Emma Café; a variety show at the Princess titled "Tantalizing Tootsies"; and a host of shooting galleries, tattoo joints, and the like. Thousands of other military personnel remain on their ship or base and listen to music, watch a movie, or write a letter to a loved one. Nearly everyone, it seems, is ready to relax, have a good time, and forget about worries and responsibilities for a while.

The date is December 6, 1941.

I am also on Oahu this night. I am a gunner's mate first class and ship's postmaster serving on a navy battleship, the USS *West Virginia*. After returning to Pearl Harbor on Friday from a thirteen-day patrol, I finished up my duties and left the ship at noon on Saturday. The harbor was packed—all eight active-duty Pacific Fleet battleships were in port, along with small craft and Coast Guard vessels, 164 ships in total. The lines at the bus stop were so long that two buses came and went before I could finally catch one and head home.

I was eager to get home. I'd married my new bride, a beautiful girl with auburn hair named Morena Holmes, on July 11. Newlyweds do not like to spend weeks apart.

We are staying with a civilian couple, Harold and Belva DeGroff, in Honolulu's Kalihi Valley. Their large home also serves as local headquarters for The Navigators, a fledgling Christian organization dedicated to spreading the message of the gospel. Harold is in charge. Morena and I are active in the movement.

Which explains why on this Saturday night, I am not at a dance, in downtown Honolulu, or otherwise occupied. The DeGroffs are taking the weekend off. I've been assigned to fill in for Harold and lead the evening meeting for more than a hundred men and women of faith, as well as a few others who've arrived to see what we are up to. The DeGroff home is built on stone piling about six feet off the ground. The huge crawl space underneath is our auditorium, complete with benches, chairs, and a sawdust floor. After a period of singing, quoting memorized Bible verses, and sharing personal stories, I deliver a brief message. Then someone gives a final prayer, and we send the crowd into the night.

It's been a time of enjoyable fellowship, a wonderful evening. None of us realize that several in our group will not live to see another day.

On Sunday morning, the aroma of fresh-cooked eggs and sizzling bacon greets me as I take a chair at the large table in the kitchen. There are eight of us—seven navy men and Joe Bodie, an army corporal who snuck away from his base last night to attend our meeting. The guys stayed over at the house to enjoy a good night's sleep and the hearty breakfast that Morena, wearing an apron, now begins to serve.

The rest of the men are in uniform, but since I'm home, I'm wearing a Hawaiian shirt. Soon I'll get dressed for church. Harold will be back home this afternoon. He'll set up the radio on the front porch, and a group of us will gather for evangelist Charles Fuller's *Old Fashioned Revival Hour*. As we listen, we'll enjoy our view of the sunshine, the heavy green foliage covering both sides of the mountains rising out of our valley, and the winding stream across the street.

I'm looking forward to it. After two weeks on patrol, nothing sounds better than a quiet day with friends and my new bride.

It is a few minutes before 8 a.m.

As I raise a fork to my mouth, the sound of a distant explosion reaches my ears. Soon there are more explosions. The army often tests gun emplacements on Sunday mornings, so the sound of heavy gunfire is not unusual. I've heard a rumor that a German battleship is in the area, as well as three British cruisers set on sinking her. I wonder if the German ship is under attack and heading for the safety of our harbor, since under international law it can remain protected in a neutral port for twenty-four hours before either surrendering or returning to battle.

As we sit at breakfast speculating, I can't resist the opportunity to needle the lone army man in our midst. "It can't be the army," I say to Joe Bodie. "They're shooting too fast." This draws a few chuckles.

Suddenly we hear the shriek of an incoming shell. It speeds over the roof and strikes in our backyard, leaving a crater that I later learn is twenty-five feet across.

All of us at the table stare at each other. Something is very wrong.

One of the navy men leaps to his feet and turns on a radio in the corner. In the next moment, Harold DeGroff appears in the doorway, his face white—he'd been on his way home and was in the yard when the shell struck.

Before Harold can speak, the voice of a Honolulu broadcaster fills the room: "I have phoned army and navy intelligence and they have advised us that the island of Oahu is under enemy attack. The enemy has not been identified. Stay tuned. We'll give more information when we get it."

There isn't time to think about who is attacking or why or what the ramifications are for America and the world. There is time only to act. I glance at Morena. "I've got to get back to the ship." I run to our bedroom, throw on my uniform. The sound of explosions is continual now. When I emerge, the radio broadcaster speaks again: "Pearl Harbor is under enemy attack. The enemy has been identified as Japan. All servicemen return to your ship or station."

A black sedan comes roaring into the driveway. Herb Goeldner, a ship-fitter first class on the USS *Argonne*, had also spent the night with us. But since he teaches a Sunday morning Bible study class on his ship, he left the house in his car a few minutes earlier. After seeing planes and bombs, he turned around and came back to pick us up.

I run out of the house, Morena close behind. Kalihi Valley is surrounded by mountains on both sides, so I can't see Pearl Harbor. What I can see is ominous black smoke filling the sky.

Two of the navy men jump into Herb's car. I stop next to the car and turn to face my wife. Will I ever see her again? I gaze into her frightened hazel eyes for the briefest moment. We kiss. Then I slide into the car.

"Deuteronomy 33:27!" Morena shouts at me. "The eternal God is your refuge, and underneath are the everlasting arms."

As Herb's car pulls away, I give Morena a little wave. She's still wearing her apron. She has tears in her eyes.

The road from our house in the valley to the harbor is lined by thick vegetation topped by coconut palm trees. Normally the picturesque journey takes less than twenty minutes. On this frantic morning, however, nothing is normal. Herb flies down the street as fast as possible, but traffic is a mess of more cars like ours, loaded with men trying to get to their posts.

As we approach, I see Japanese planes diving at the harbor. "Where are *our* planes?" cries Ken Watters, a yeoman on the admiral's staff on the *Maryland*. I hear the mixture of anger and anguish in his voice.

We finally reach the base gate where Marine Harold Blakeslee, another fellow Navigator, waves us through. I learn later than Blakeslee is lucky to still be standing; a strafer's bullet has gone through the cuff of his pants.

We park, pile out of the car, and run to the boat landing at Merry Point, located just south of the office of Admiral Husband E. Kimmel, commander in chief of the Pacific Fleet. When I look past Kuahua Peninsula to Ford Island and "Battleship Row," where the *West Virginia* and the rest of our finest warships are moored, I am shocked.

Everywhere the Japanese have struck us, there is devastation and horror.

The *Oklahoma* is upside down. The *Arizona* is belching black smoke and red flames like a volcano. The *West Virginia*, which we crewmen affectionately call the "Wee Vee," is sinking and on fire above the waterline. The first wave of the attack has ended, but enemy planes still zigzag across the sky, their crews seeking to inflict further damage. The air is heavy with the odor of gunpowder mixed with smoke.

I know in that moment that many of my shipmates and friends are already dead.

I have always appreciated history. I am aware that the Japanese have employed the tactic of surprise attack before, in 1904, against the Russian fleet. Rage wells up inside me. I can't believe we've allowed them to do it to us.

The motor launches that would normally take us to Ford Island and to our ships aren't running. They're too busy trying to pick up men who've either jumped or been blown by bombs into the water. I can't see it just yet, but the water surrounding our battleships is covered by a layer of oil spilling out from gaping holes in the ships. The oil is on fire. The men who've gone overboard are burning alive.

Ken Watters and I have both arrived carrying our Bibles and notebooks, ready to do spiritual battle as well as naval warfare. Then it occurs to Ken that books may not be practical at the moment. "Looks like we're going to need both hands," he says. I spot a fire extinguisher rack at the boat landing. We store our materials there.

A few more navy men join us at the dock. Our group of about ten decides to strike out on foot for the ferry landing across the water from the south end of Ford Island. We begin walking rapidly in that direction, our ears bombarded by the constant drone of Japanese planes flying overhead and by the punctuated bursts of our own antiaircraft guns.

Suddenly the sound of a single engine overpowers the rest.

A plane is bearing down on our group. It dives at us from an angle and banks, startlingly low, perhaps forty feet above the ground and eighty feet away. It's olive drab in color, so for an instant I think it's one of ours.

The image freezes in my mind—the cockpit cover off, the pilot, goggles on, focused, so close that even his eyes and teeth are visible, smoke emitting from the machine guns.

I drop to the ground at the same time that the sound of machine-gun fire reaches my ears.

The plane roars past. I turn my head. The plane levels out, revealing a rising sun under its wing. On the dirt road behind me, dust rises from a trench dug by bullets.

I have had no hatred of the Japanese. I am a Christian. I know the Bible and the verses that say to love your enemy. I believe wholeheartedly in God and in the wisdom of following his instructions.

Still, the instinct to survive is a strong one, one of our strongest. This war just became personal. My enemy has just tried to kill me.

If he comes back, I will defend myself. If I have to, I will shoot him dead.

★ 1 ★

DREAMS AND SHADOWS

A WISP OF SMOKE and the sizzles and snaps of a crackling fire emanated from a huge wood stove in the center of the room. Seven men were gathered on "loafer's benches" around the inviting warmth, most with a pipe protruding from one corner of their mouths and a wad of chewing tobacco in the other. The men were in their fifties and sixties, wore overalls, and had beards and unruly hair in dire need of a barber's scissors. Every few moments, one or two in the group let loose a stream of tobacco juice in the direction of a two-foot-wide spittoon near the stove. They missed as often as they hit their target.

The men were not alone. I was there too, a four-year-old boy wearing a homemade blue denim shirt and overalls. I sat on the lap of one man for several minutes until I was gently passed on, one lap to the next, welcomed by each of the men into their circle. I listened and tried to understand as the "loafers" discussed issues of the day. It was October 1917.

My father, Claude Casey (C. C.) Downing, owned the country store in my hometown of Plevna, Missouri, population 110. Since my father and my mother, Estelle Downing, both worked at the store, I spent most of my preschool days there as well. Our store was more than a business: The thirty-by-eighty-foot building with tall windows across the front and a hitching post for horses on the side served as one of our town's social centers—especially for the regulars who gathered each day around the stove. I was a silent member of the Spit and Argue Club, as the men were known. I loved it.

The primary topic of conversation on this day was the state of the war in Europe. It seems that from my earliest days, the military ambitions of the world's nations and the men who led them were a presence looming over my life.

The Great War officially began in 1914. I'd been born eleven months before at my family's home in Oak Grove, Missouri, a small town on the eastern outskirts of Kansas City. My great uncle, Dr. Jim Downing, did the honors, ushering me into the world on August 22, 1913. Apparently my parents were so grateful that they named me after him. My middle name, Willis, came from my mother's father and grandfather, Willis Anderson Jr. and Willis Anderson Sr.

With my birth, our family expanded to five. Besides my parents, I joined my sister, Dorothy (four years older) and my brother Donald (two years older). My younger brother, A. J., was born two years after me. At the time of my arrival, I doubt my parents and siblings had war on their minds, but others in the world must have seen it coming. An arms race and complex alliances among European nations, combined with conflict in the Balkans, made an outbreak of hostilities increasingly likely. The assassination in Sarajevo of Archduke Franz Ferdinand, heir to the throne of Austria-Hungary, ignited the deadly conflict.

My companions at the store, along with the vast majority of Americans, had favored staying out of the matter. Isolationism, they said, had served the country well since the days of George Washington and would continue to do so. Our greatest allies in the world, it was thought, were the Atlantic and Pacific Oceans.

But Germany's aggressive U-boat campaign, which took US lives with the sinking of the passenger liner RMS *Lusitania*, combined with news of an intercepted German message inviting Mexico to join in a war against America, proved too provoking for the nation to stay neutral. On April 6, 1917, Congress declared war on Germany and began sending materials and men to assist the Allies.

Six months later, the Spit and Argue Club now gathered around the stove debating the progress of the war with an intensity that did not match their otherwise laid-back appearance and kindly nature. Though I didn't understand it then, their depth of feeling was not surprising. Plevna had been founded only a generation earlier by immigrants from Bulgaria. The scope of the war included the homeland of my older friends. It was being fought by their relatives.

Though I did not follow all that was said, the conversations that passed just over my head between discharges of tobacco juice had a great influence on me. My companions were unanimously and unequivocally against "the Germans," blaming them for starting the war. I'd recently begun hearing the terms *Germans* and *germs*; I took them both to mean the same thing—something very bad.

In addition to gaining my first appreciation for the toil and toll of war, I suspect that I also acquired my contrary nature and passion for debate from these men. My mother may have suspected it too, for she made it clear she did not consider the loafers to be favorable role models. Theirs looked like a pretty good life to me, however, and I made plans to join their ranks as soon as possible.

My family's move from Oak Grove to Plevna was the result of a gift. After my parents married, my mother's parents gave them sixty acres of land near their Plevna-area home. They hoped the land would keep us close by. My father bought a custom kit for $2,500 and built a three-bedroom home there that overlooked acres of virgin timber to the east. To the north were the Little Fabius River and a valley that included rich, black soil, ideal for farming.

But Dad, well-educated and ambitious, wasn't destined to be a farmer. He soon sold much of the land, rented a house for fifteen dollars a month, and purchased the hardware store on the dirt road that was Plevna's main street.

We offered just about everything at our store that a Plevna citizen might need: guns and ammunition, dry goods and groceries, clothing, drugs, and home remedies. Farmers brought in chickens, eggs, rabbits, cream, and other items that they sold to my father to raise cash for their purchases.

The store also housed the Plevna post office. As the store owner, my father followed tradition by serving as postmaster. The US Post Office Department furnished stamps and authorized my father to keep the income from their sales as his salary. Technically it was against the law for anyone but my father to enter the postal enclosure in the corner of the store, but everyone in our family took a turn there, selling stamps and other items. When evenings at the store wore on and I got sleepy, I opened the door to the postal section, made a bed of the stack of empty mail sacks, and slept until my mother awakened me and took me home.

Life in Plevna was primitive by today's standards, though we never saw it that way. The average home, including ours, had no indoor plumbing. It was traditional to take a Saturday-night bath. The facility for this was a tin washtub, thirty inches in diameter. By each Friday, the combination of wearing underclothing, long johns, and the same socks for a week produced a noticeable supply of "toe jam." Other sanitary duties required a trip to the outhouse.

In addition to operating the store and post office, my father served as president of the local bank he had founded, earning a salary of ninety dollars a month. My brothers and I supplemented this income by trapping muskrats, which sold for $1.15 per pelt. Once, I found I'd caught a mink instead of a muskrat. The $18.50 I received for the mink pelt was just enough to cover the cost of a new coat.

Most of the rest of the population of Plevna worked hard to

make a living as farmers. The main crops in our area were corn, oats, and timothy hay, as well as wheat and specialized crops such as "kafir corn," a popcorn-like grain. The men plowed and harrowed the soil, then planted their seeds in the spring (or fall, in the case of wheat). The first stage of harvesting began about four months later.

Oats, timothy, and wheat had to be threshed to separate the grain from the pods in which it grew. The farmers mowed the standing grain with a horse-drawn machine called a binder, which tied the stalks into bundles ten inches in diameter. Laborers followed the binder and neatly stacked the bundles in round piles with the grain at the top. These architecturally perfect piles were called shocks. The grain dried out in four to six weeks, by the middle of August.

Threshing day was the farm event of the year. Every community owned a threshing machine made up of two distinct units. The first was a steam engine that looked like a small locomotive. It turned a flywheel, three feet in diameter. The second unit was a separator, a large tin box on wheels that was twenty feet long, eight feet high, and five feet wide. Inside the box was a sophisticated series of belts and rotating iron axles with lugs and spikes to pound the grain from its pod. The separator was powered by a belt from the steam-engine flywheel.

On threshing day, a man wielding a pitchfork tore down the shocks and spread the bundles to dry out the morning dew. A little later, more men arrived to load the bundles onto wagons and transport them to the thresher. As the bundles were fed into the threshing machine, a line of wagons stood ready to receive the grain and haul it to the barn or granary.

My brothers and I sometimes volunteered to help tear down the shocks, but we had an ulterior motive. We liked to capture nonvenomous snakes living in the shocks, which we would then tie to the bundle with twine we carried for just that purpose. When a farmer arrived to toss the bundles onto his wagon with a pitchfork, he inevitably came to one we'd specially prepared. The result was great entertainment for the Downing brothers. As the bundle and wiggling snake flew through the air, the farmer would try to knock the snake down, not knowing it was tied to the bundle. The poor snake would jump in every direction, trying to escape.

I am not aware that anyone ever discovered our plot. If they had, I might not be here today.

Threshing day was a community enterprise. The separator and steam engine moved from farm to farm until everyone's grain was threshed. It didn't matter if the farm was large or small. The objective was to get everyone's threshing done before the fall rains came. No money changed hands between farmers. They and the other men in the community exchanged labor freely, joyfully, and competitively to see who could do the most for someone else.

Women exhibited the same cooperative and enthusiastic spirit. While the men were in the field, their wives gathered at the home of the host to prepare a meal unrivaled for quality, quantity, and variety. These women brought their finest canned goods and used their favorite recipes to create a banquet of fried chicken, smoked ham, sweet corn, mashed potatoes, sweet potatoes, cooked and fresh tomatoes, and fresh peas and beans. The feast was supplemented with lettuce, radishes, cantaloupe, watermelon, preserved pears, and dried apples and peaches. For drink, the wives served iced tea and lemonade, and for dessert they offered blackberry, gooseberry, cherry, lemon, custard, rhubarb, apple, peach, mincemeat, pumpkin, and chocolate pies topped with real whipped cream, as well as every kind of cake, covered with thick icing and coconut.

The big meal was served at noon. When the dinner bell rang, the field laborers came to the house to water their horses and gorge themselves. After the meal, they lay down in the shade for half an hour, then continued threshing until darkness fell.

I spent a week every summer at my grandparents' farm. I always hoped my visit would coincide with threshing season. When it did, I rode in the grain wagon and buried my bare feet in the sweet-smelling mass of wheat kernels. At noon I ate until I couldn't sit up straight. My favorites were the fried chicken and custard pies. I was thankful to not be a city boy.

It seems that in America today we take great pride in our independence. But in those days we had to depend on each other. The attitude was, "I'll help you, you help me." If you needed to borrow a piece of machinery or a horse, you asked a neighbor. As far as I know, no one was ever turned down. If one family knew of another in need, someone—usually the wife—would take an item off the shelf at home and give it to them, as quietly as possible so as not to embarrass the family. That was just the way things worked.

We also bartered. Not every small community enjoyed such services, but Plevna was blessed by the presence of Dr. John Hayden, a country doctor. Dr. Hayden never had an office. He went where the people were and was available twenty-four hours a day. His patients often did not have money to reimburse him, however. Instead of cash, people would give him a jar of jam, vegetables from the garden, or some other item as payment. This is why Dr. Hayden's home looked like a grocery store.

Dr. Hayden didn't mind. After all, he wasn't trying to get rich, and he always had something to eat.

This spirit of interdependence and cooperation extended to our churches. There were three in Plevna: Methodist, Disciples of Christ, and the one we attended, Southern Baptist. They were far apart in doctrine, yet they operated as one for community projects. The churches rotated the annual Christmas party, each one hosting all of the town's children. They also rotated summer revival meetings. Our churches set the moral tone for Plevna both spiritually and socially, exploiting what they had in common rather than their differences.

Our community was not flawless. We had our share of small-time criminals, and it was common knowledge as to who was having an affair with whom. But people had their way of dealing with these issues. They shunned the criminals and accepted without stigma the children who were thought to be illegitimate. The system may have been imperfect, but it seemed to work.

The Great War ended when Germany signed an armistice with the Allies on November 11, 1918. I was five years old. At the outset of the war, President Woodrow Wilson had declared that "the world must be made safe for democracy." People across the country were now declaring that mission accomplished. My memory of the local people's reaction is that they were just glad the handful of boys from our community could come home.

My friends in the Spit and Argue Club moved on to other topics. A year later, I moved on as well, when I started first grade.

My teacher was a short woman with brown hair—straight on the sides, bangs in front—that made her head look square. She was a wonderful person. I've often said that the highest compliment a student can pay his teacher is to still remember her name a few years after completing the class. After nearly a century, I still recall the name of Beulah Foster—as well as the names of the rest of my Plevna teachers.

We children were expected to sit in our desks, face the blackboard, and pay attention. The Plevna school was a one-room operation with a partition dividing high school students from the rest of the grades. Two teachers handled the duties on each side. In grades one through eight, we never had more than five or six students per class on our side of the building, while the high school enrolled twenty at the most.

Our instructional materials were limited to a huge dictionary, a globe of the world, some maps on the wall, and a set of encyclopedias. We studied the basics: reading, writing, and 'rithmetic. Current events in the nation and world were rarely discussed because we had little knowledge of them. You could say that we were isolated.

In late fall and early winter, the dirt roads around Plevna got so muddy that no one could leave town until the mud froze. We did have two weekly newspapers, the *Edina Sentinel* and *Knox County Democrat*. These mostly reported local stories about everyone's health and who was visiting whom. Thanks to my father, we also had mail service at two cents for a letter and a penny for a postcard. Otherwise, our communication with the outside world depended on the telephone and word of mouth.

Mrs. Hannah Luckett was the Plevna switchboard operator, which she ran from her home. When a call came from the outside world, Mrs. Luckett patched a line on her switchboard between the caller and the intended recipient. Almost every home had a phone, a creation mounted on the wall with two bells at the top and a microphone that protruded from the middle, resembling Pinocchio's nose. The overall effect was of a robot with giant eyes. To make a call, the originator picked up the receiver and turned a hand crank, which sent a signal to a central switchboard.

It was too expensive for families to own an individual line, so six to eight homes shared a line. Since outside news was limited, it was generally assumed that no matter whose phone was called, others on the party line were listening in and might even participate in the conversation.

During nearly every thunderstorm, lightning struck the telephone lines somewhere. To protect the instruments inside homes from being burned out, every house had a quick release hook for disconnecting the line when a storm was brewing. Reconnecting the line was a hazardous act. I was probably seven years old the first time I was assigned this duty. I went just outside the front door in my bare feet, stood in the wet grass, and grasped the end of one wire in my left hand and the other wire in my right, making my body a handy electrical conductor.

Naturally, someone on our party line chose that moment to place a call. I'd been warned that I might feel a "tickle" when I put the wires together. The feeling was closer to a football tackle. The voltage generated by the powerful magneto produced a shock so strong that I could not let go of the wires until the caller finally stopped cranking. I was not electrocuted, but the sensation was remarkably and uncomfortably close.

My school years coincided with the Roaring Twenties. For city dwellers in America and around the world, this meant jazz music, women known as flappers, the age of the automobile, and unprecedented economic growth. Some of these exciting changes even reached our tiny community. Our grandfather purchased a 1911 Ford Model T, which I began driving at the age of eleven. I couldn't see over the steering wheel, so I guided the car by looking out the side. Our cars were designed for open touring. The public was slow to accept the glassed-in sedan as they considered glass a death warrant if there was an accident.

The Twenties was also the era of Prohibition, a nationwide ban on the sale and production of alcoholic beverages. It was also the era of the gangsters, who defied and exploited the new law. One day I was driving to school on the highway when I spotted a big limousine in the distance ahead of me. The limo driver had taken a corner too fast on the slick road and slid into the ditch. As I approached, a man in a fashionable black suit and cap was trying to push the limo back onto the road. Another man sat at the wheel.

I pulled to a stop in front of them. "Need some help?" I called.

The men examined me for a moment, hard expressions on their faces. "No thanks," the one in back said.

But I was already out of my Model T and walking toward the back of the limo. When I reached the rear doors, I noticed that white sheets inside the car blocked the windows. Curious, I stopped and peeked behind a small opening between the sheets. Mounted inside the rear of the car was a pair of Thompson submachine guns.

I felt a hand on my back, pushing me firmly away from the window and toward the back of the vehicle. It was the man in the black suit and cap. He didn't say anything, but his expression was even harder than before.

I helped push the car back onto the road. Without a word, the man in the suit got into the limo's passenger seat and the two men drove off. It wasn't until I was back in my car and again on my way to school that I realized these men were gangsters, probably on their way from Chicago to Kansas City to fulfill a contract.

There were other technological advances in addition to automobiles. In 1916, radio pioneer David Sarnoff predicted that homes all over America would one day be equipped with radio music boxes that would tune in news, information, and entertainment sent out by wireless from central broadcasting points. His prophecy was realized in the early 1920s.

My father saw the potential of home radio and secured the exclusive distributorship for our region. We immediately had more customers than we could handle. I often went with my dad to set up a home radio, a two-hour task. Each radio was so heavy it took both of us to carry it.

As radios improved, a large, phonograph-like speaker was added. We used it in our store to hear the broadcast of the controversial "long count" heavyweight championship fight won by Gene Tunney over Jack Dempsey in 1927. We also listened to baseball's World Series. In 1926 and 1928, we rooted for our St. Louis Cardinals, led by Rogers Hornsby and Dizzy Dean, to defeat the powerhouse New York Yankees, led by Babe Ruth and Lou Gehrig (the Cardinals did win in '26). Our favorite radio program, though, featured the entertaining escapades of Amos and Andy.

We did have skeptics in the neighborhood. One farmer insisted that nothing could come out of that box that had not been put in it. He went to his grave believing radio was a hoax and that there was a hidden record somewhere inside.

Through radio, we had far greater access to news of the world. I paid little attention, though, to reports of the creation of the Communist party in China in 1921, the establishment of the Union of Soviet Socialist Republics (USSR) in 1922, and increasing domestic problems in Japan. Like my elders and most Americans, I trusted our government to monitor these matters.

I had a good life. Most anything our family wanted was in stock at the store, and we simply took it off the shelf as needed. In those days before sales and income taxes, my father never kept books. If I needed a nickel, a dime, or even a quarter, I took one out of the money drawer.

Moreover, everything seemed possible in the Twenties. The nation was at peace and most people seemed to be making money. I enjoyed reading about the adventures of Lou Wetzel and Betty Zane in Zane Grey westerns and imagined myself as a cowboy. I also read Horatio Alger books. The Alger plots, as I recall, were always similar: a country boy goes to the city; he meets a benefactor to whom he demonstrates the virtues of honesty, reliability, and hard work; he is rewarded with a good job and goes on to become a prominent citizen in the community. These stories built up in me a belief in myself and the idea that displaying such virtues would surely lead to success.

I don't know if it was the times, the Alger books, or something I inherited from my motivated father, but ambition began to bubble up within me. I was nine or ten and studying a civics book at school when I read that any American citizen could become president of the United States.

I thought, *Well, I'm a citizen. Why don't I run for it?*

In that moment, I set the presidency as my life goal. I would keep my eyes fixed on that prize for the next twelve years.

My growing ambition and self-confidence, perhaps combined with memories of my membership in the Spit and Argue Club, must have made me precocious. When I was twelve, I took an old wagon chassis and built a bed for it. During threshing season, when the farmers gathered the shocks in their huge wagons, I brought out my wagon and joined them. None of the other kids did that. The farmers seemed to appreciate my help and treated me almost as an equal.

Unlike my contemporaries, I often started conversations with my elders and attempted to relate to them as equals. Later, after I entered high school, I found myself conversing with Mr. Fred Spees, the principal, about history, philosophy, politics, and the war. I had a strong curiosity about life, the world, and how we all fit into it. Mr. Spees liked me and seemed to enjoy our discussions.

I regularly went to church, but my faith held little meaning for me. I only gave the appearance that high morals were important to me. I didn't want to do anything that would get me into trouble or put me in jail—not because I felt doing such things was wrong, but because I knew it would be bad for my reputation and hold me back from my goals. So, when friends began gambling money on our games of marbles, I quit. When some of my acquaintances smoked cigarettes and drank liquor, I stayed away from them.

By the time I achieved the age of sixteen, I thought the future for one James Willis Downing was very bright indeed. I even bragged about the fact that I expected one day to serve in the White House.

Then came September 1929. The US stock market began to wobble, exposing the nation's economic vulnerability. On October 24, the market lost 11 percent of its value at the opening bell. A rally briefly calmed some panicked investors, but then the market fell 13 percent on October 28 and another 12 percent on October 29—"Black Tuesday." These events were a spreading dark cloud that would have ominous implications for the nation and the world, eventually casting their shadow over famine, despair, opportunism, and finally, a return to war. They would also dramatically change the direction of my life, putting me on a course I had never imagined.

It was the beginning of the Great Depression.

★ 2 ★

THE REAL WORLD

A CITY WAS NOT THE PLACE to be during the first years of the Depression. As stock values continued to drop during the early 1930s, businesses failed. The unemployment rate rose from 3.2 percent in 1929 to 23.6 percent in 1932—nearly one in four workers was out of a job. Banks failed and life savings disappeared, leaving many Americans destitute. With no job and no savings, thousands of Americans lost their homes. The poor congregated in "Hoovervilles" made up of tents and crate-and-cardboard shacks in cities across the nation. Thousands suffered from hunger and malnutrition.

Those of us in Plevna were in better shape. Farmers were a self-sufficient bunch. Nearly everyone had a large garden and chickens, hogs, and sheep that could be butchered for weeks of choice meat. Wives canned and stockpiled fruit and other goods. Bartering increased. People joined beef clubs—eight families would put their money together to buy a steer and divide the meat into eighths, rotating the parts the next time. No one owned a refrigerator, but our winters were cold enough that we simply hung the meat on the back porch. When it was time to cook dinner, my mother used a meat saw to cut off what she needed.

Our family was better off than most. My father had sold the store by this time and taken a position as president of the local bank, so he had a steady income. But cash was in short supply for everyone. When clothes wore out or a buggy or horse needed replacing, people had to do without. Yet everyone still needed items like sugar and flour, so they found a way to pay for them. Sometimes they resorted to desperate measures. The cooperative spirit remained alive in Plevna, and families continued to look out for one another. But some who needed help were too proud to ask. The result was an increase in thievery.

Chickens were the easiest product to turn into cash, making late-night chicken raids a common occurrence. One morning I was checking on my grandparents' farm and noticed that quite a few chickens were missing. The corncrib had been broken into. I played amateur detective and discovered tire prints at the front gate—three Goodyear tires with a diamond tread, and one Fisk tire with a dotted tread. A few days later I spotted a car with the same distribution of tires. My father spoke to the owner of the business where the car was parked. The businessman checked under the car's backseat and observed several grains of corn.

We were sure we'd found the culprits, but we didn't pursue

the matter further. They were relatives. We knew they'd fallen on hard times and needed cash.

I'm sorry to say there were times I decided I needed a little extra cash myself, even if it was at the expense of others. Because of my seemingly high moral standards and popularity among the adults, I was named treasurer of my Sunday school class. Each week I took the offering in class. After church, I took the money home and put it in a glass jar in my bedroom. At the end of each month, I deposited the collection of dimes, nickels, and pennies in the bank.

Our church leaders overestimated my character at the time, however. My parents had allocated me lunch money of a dime a day. Occasionally, when I felt a dime wasn't sufficient, I supplemented it with a coin from the offering jar. The church's total contributions to my midday meals probably added up to a couple of dollars, a nice sum back then. When I eventually confessed to my actions, my mother replaced the funds and gave me a stern lecture.

By the time I reached high school age, I had also developed a bad habit of "forgetting" some debts. Each weekday I drove our Model T to school and back. Naturally the generator, spark plugs, and other parts eventually wore out. If one's reputation was good enough, one could go into a business and say he didn't have enough cash at the moment but would pay up eventually, and walk out with whatever item he needed. I did it myself when I needed a part for the Model T. In a few cases at the town's general store across the street from our old store, I pretended to not remember that I still owed the store money. Later, after I became a Christian, I went back to repay my debt.

The business owners had long ago forgotten what I owed, but I had not. It was a humiliating but important step in my faith.

My family moved to my grandparents' farm before my junior year of high school. We bought a Farmall tractor and became full-fledged farmers. During crop-planting time, my brothers and I got up at daylight and worked in the field until it was time to drive to school. After school we resumed our farm work, sometimes keeping at it until late at night with the help of the tractor's lights.

In 1931, the education authorities in Plevna decided they weren't qualified to instruct senior high school students, so I enrolled at Novelty High for my final year. It was ten miles away. Our senior class was thirty-four students.

Three of my classmates also commuted to Novelty. One of them was a girl named LaVaughn Dingle. Her father owned a gas station and provided gas for the car as payment for me to transport her to school. She was sweet on another boy who commuted and wanted her parents to arrange for her to ride with him, but she was stuck with me. She was short and pretty, with long, light brown hair, but there was no chance of a romance. LaVaughn disliked me immensely.

At the noon hour, I drove my school friends to the drugstore a quarter mile away. We paid fifteen cents for a tenderloin sandwich and a cold drink. I must have been a bit of a showoff, because on the trips back I learned how to approach the dirt parking spot in front of the school at moderate speed, slam on the brakes, and turn the wheel sharply, causing the back end of the car to slide. As the dust flew, I guided the Model T into the parking space backward with the precision of a race car driver.

Academics came easy to me, so I didn't study much. I enjoyed competing on the debate team and usually defended the most contrary opinion, perhaps another influence of the Spit and Argue Club. I showed my innovative side by rounding up a few friends and creating a makeshift tennis court on one friend's spare land. The six or eight of us who played called ourselves the Rinky Dink Club, after a popular comic strip.

I also competed in school athletics, lettering in both basketball and track and field. My events in the latter were the high jump, one-hundred-yard dash, discus, and shot put. Our coach was apparently unsatisfied with the performance of some of my teammates, so he recruited me to also try the javelin. He showed me how to hold and release the spear. Neither of us realized what starting the Model T with a hand crank every day had done for the muscles in my right arm and shoulder. My first throw went ten yards over the heads of those who had been measuring the other athletes' throws. I eventually won an award in the javelin at the county track and field meet.

Graduation day was approaching. My grades were not the highest in the class, but Mr. Spees selected me to be valedictorian anyway. He gave me a typed, two-page valedictory address to memorize. I still remember the opening lines: "Foremost among the ideals which have characterized our national existence is the spirit of self-reliance." I suspect these words had been used often for inspirational addresses. The graduation ceremony took place on the Novelty basketball court, which doubled as the auditorium. My speech received an enthusiastic round of applause. Only Mr. Spees and I knew I didn't write it.

My senior year of high school had ended in a blaze of glory. Now I was in the real world. I knew where I wanted to end up—the White House—but how was I going to get there?

Job openings in the summer of 1932 were rare indeed, and my experience was limited. I had worked for money three times as a farm laborer during hay harvest season, twice earning a dollar and once earning $1.25 for twelve-hour days. When elementary school teachers got sick, the school authorities recruited high school students to fill in, so I'd also earned a few dollars as a substitute teacher.

My brother and sister were both college graduates, yet the only way they could make any money was by selling apples and pencils on the street corner. Teaching seemed the only profession where I might be able to earn a living.

I heard about a teaching opening in a local country school and applied for the job. The school board president gave me a perfunctory interview, but he had already decided to hire a girl in their community.

I was nearly nineteen years old and facing an uncertain future. I had big aspirations and a philosophy I'd derived from a poem I'd read. I believed I would find fulfillment by being able to say at the end of the day, "I've lived today. If tomorrow is as good as today I will have no complaints." The trouble was that I wasn't too sure my tomorrows were going to be as good. The nation's prospects, as well as my own, seemed bleak.

In the midst of this fog, a beacon of hope appeared. Curtis, a Plevna classmate who'd graduated two years ahead of me, came home that summer riding a big Harley-Davidson motorcycle he'd purchased. Curtis had joined the navy; he was now a third class electrician on a submarine.

In my view, Curtis was a successful capitalist. His base pay, in addition to room and board and medical and dental care, was ninety dollars a month. That was the same salary my dad made as president of the bank, which supported a family of six.

The navy began to look like my best option. Military service was part of my family history, after all. Two of my great-grandfathers had fought in the Civil War—one for the North and one for the South. I envisioned serving in the navy for four years and saving enough money to attend college and then law school. After that I would go into politics and begin my climb to the presidency.

A friend, Donald Humphrey, and I drove southeast to Hannibal, which had the closest navy recruitment station. The recruiter gave us a thorough physical examination, followed by a rigorous written exam. Because of the Depression, the navy was besieged with applications. Typically, accepted recruits had to wait six to eight months before induction. I figured if I was fortunate enough to get on a waiting list, I'd have a few months to seek additional opportunities and then choose what seemed best for me.

The verdict after our exams was that Donald was underweight and would not be considered. He could put on a few pounds and come back later. At nearly six feet and 162 pounds, however, I was in "perfect physical condition." I needed only one tooth filling. My exam score was 98, the second highest the excited recruiter had ever seen. He said he was putting me (and the man who'd scored 100 percent) at the top of his list.

The good news came in September. I was to be inducted into the navy later in the month.

On September 21, 1932—I was nineteen years and thirty days old—I left for Hannibal with my dad. Saying good-bye at home was hard on my mother. Both my parents had faced economic reality and approved of my decision, but my mother shed many tears nonetheless.

At Hannibal, the navy recruiter met us and put me up in a cheap hotel. I said good-bye to my dad. He was not a man given to speeches or displays of affection, yet he hugged me and wished me well. He had hoped to join the navy himself out of college but had decided to marry my mother instead. I now saw in his eyes that he was proud of me for having the courage to strike out on my own.

When my dad left, I was alone. For the first time in my life I was removed from the security of my family.

My hotel room was spare. There was no bath, no air con-ditioning, no phone or other amenity. That evening I turned off the lights and lay in bed, my eyes wide open. The recruiter was to pick me up early in the morning and put me on a train for the six-hour ride to St. Louis, where I was to be sworn in. Since I had no watch, I worried that I would sleep in and miss the train.

I needn't have worried. I couldn't sleep.

The navy's recruiting slogan at the time was, "Join the navy and see the world." After living my entire life in rural Missouri, that idea excited me. I had an adventurous spirit and was ready to expand my horizons. Of course there was the possibility that I would have to defend my country. If I made a career of the navy, I was bound to see at least one war. But America had been at peace for fourteen years. Such dangers seemed remote that night in Hannibal.

It was a turning point in my life and I knew it. The world was waiting for me. A new adventure was about to begin.

I did make the train in the morning. In St. Louis, I was taken to the navy recruiting center, where about thirty of us lined up to be sworn in. "If you don't want to join the navy," the recruiter warned, "decide so now. After you take this oath you are in the navy. You can be put in jail for desertion if you change your mind."

It was sobering to hear those words, but I had no doubts. I'd resolved that this was the path to my future. Nothing would stop me now.

We rode an overnight train to Great Lakes, Illinois, about forty miles north of Chicago. A bus took us to Camp Berry, a recruit training facility. The first thing I remember of the place was a trip to the barbershop. We were hustled in and out as if we were on an assembly line. After about six passes with a barber's electric clippers, the shape of each of our heads was revealed to the world. A small, Indian brave–like tuft was all that remained of our former head covering.

A few of the recruits had beautiful, long hair. When they took their seats, the barber sometimes ran his fingers through their shaggy manes. "Do you want to keep this?" he asked. If the answer was yes, the barber said, "Hold out your hands." The barber enjoyed his joke more than we recruits did.

Next came a visit to the clothing outfitters. From experience, the navy knew that with a regular diet and sleep the average recruit would gain eight to ten pounds. After a quick measure of chest, waist, and leg length, I staggered away with about seventy pounds of clothing, none of which fit me at that moment. We were given two options for our civilian clothes—donate them to charity or ship them home. I sent mine home but never wore them again. The navy was right—I gained close to eight pounds in eight weeks.

I joined about 230 recruits in Great Lakes for training. Two companies of one hundred men each were formed. The latest arrivals—me included—were left over. We were placed in a "drag company," which meant we would have to wait for the next month's arrivals before beginning formal training. After three weeks of quarantine to weed out any infectious diseases, the thirty of us were merged with a new group into Company 6. We spent hours each day on the Camp Berry field in infantry drill. The purpose was to engender teamwork and instill discipline, then defined as "prompt, cheerful, and complete obedience to all orders received."

Drill starts without a rifle but progresses to formations with rifles and bayonets. When the order is given, "To the rear, march," the man who fails to reverse direction finds himself being trampled by riflemen with bayonets fixed. I learned quickly to listen carefully and obey.

My introduction to firing a .30-30 Springfield rifle was equally painful. On a bitterly cold day at the rifle range, I aimed my weapon toward Lake Michigan and pulled the trigger. Since I had fired only light weapons, I held the rifle rather loosely. The recoil from my first shot spun me around and left me with a bruised shoulder. I discovered that the rifle butt must be pressed tight against flesh and bone to prevent severe bruising. It seemed I was learning most of my navy lessons the hard way.

Yet my training did eventually take hold. After Christmas, my company mates and I graduated from Camp Berry. I was promoted to seaman second class, with a base pay of thirty-six dollars a month.

That soon changed, however. After his March inauguration, one of the first acts of our new president, Franklin Delano Roosevelt, was to cut the pay of government employees by 15 percent. My salary was reduced to $30.60 per month.

On assignment day, about two hundred of us lined up ten feet away from a bulletin board. The board had a sign-up sheet for each ship that needed men, along with only enough lines for the number of men who would be allotted per ship. When a whistle blew, we were to rush forward and sign our names to the sheet and ship we wanted.

The thirty of us in drag company had formed a friendship and decided we wanted to go to the same ship—our newest battleship, the USS *West Virginia*. We formed a flying wedge and pushed off the other sailors while one of our group signed all thirty of our names on the sheet.

A few days later, a fifty-foot motor launch carried me and all my possessions—packed into one "sea bag"—through the waves to the battleship that would become my new home. The

West Virginia was stationed in Long Beach, California. It was midmorning on Friday, March 10, 1933.

I was topside at just before 6 p.m. that day. The ship suddenly began to vibrate so violently that for fifteen seconds it was difficult to stand. The eighty-pound-per-link anchor chain bounced up and down as if it were made of rope. The word spread that our gun magazines had blown up. When we looked ashore, though, we could see fires breaking out all over the city. Even from a mile away we could hear the sirens of ambulances, fire trucks, and police vehicles.

The cause was a 6.3-magnitude earthquake centered fifteen miles south of Long Beach. The disaster killed 115 people, the most deadly California quake since more than three thousand perished in and around San Francisco in 1906. Instead of enjoying California, I was kept on the ship for six weeks while cleanup from the earthquake took place.

Perhaps naval service was going to be a bit more dangerous than I'd thought.

The *West Virginia* was an impressive ship, longer than two football fields and capable of twenty-one knots (twenty-four miles per hour). It was armed with eight .45-caliber guns, each sixteen inches in diameter; eight five-inch, .51-caliber guns; and eight five-inch, .25-caliber antiaircraft guns. What most impressed this boy from small-town Plevna, however, was how crowded the ship was. Fifteen hundred sailors and officers, all sharing the same living space. There were people everywhere.

Living in close quarters with so many men made showers

and a daily change into clean clothes a priority. Shower instructions were posted in the community washrooms:

Wet Down Your Body With Fresh Water.
Turn Off Fresh Water Shower.
Lather Up Your Body With Soap.
Rinse Off With Salt Water.

The procedure for washing clothes was equally regimented. Outside the washroom, a few dozen of us undressed, put our white clothes in a galvanized bucket, and inserted our ration of two gallons of fresh water. Next we slid the bucket over a steam pipe and turned up the steam until the water boiled. Then we used the same water to wash dark clothes. After a rinse with cold saltwater, we hung up the clothes to dry anyplace we could find. The ship's interior was always warm and often hot, so it did the job.

Staying clean was not our mission, however. A battleship exists to shoot its guns at another ship or a land target. Its crew exists to train, shoot, and maintain the ship for battle. I was assigned to the second division, turret two, which housed two sixteen-inch guns on the forward part of the ship. Each gun barrel weighed 105 tons and required five hundred pounds of powder per gun to send a two-thousand-pound projectile up to twenty-one miles to its target.

My first battle station was in the lower powder-handling room. Powder bags and the projectile from the shell deck were delivered to the breech of the gun by a series of hoists and hydraulic lifts. About ninety men were required to fire the guns.

I soon had a different responsibility: firing pointer. This meant I coached two other sailors to line up the vertical and horizontal crosshairs on their telescopes. When I was satisfied we were on target, I was the person who actually pulled the trigger.

My first experience was traumatic. The guns had to be pointed broadside to absorb the recoil and keep from damaging the ship. Even so, every shot caused our huge battleship to skid twenty feet sideways. When I pulled the trigger, the noise and vibration were so severe I thought I'd blown up the ship. All I could see through my telescope was smoke. I assumed I'd somehow made a horrible error and that we were sinking. But as the smoke cleared, I observed that our target a mile away had two holes in its center.

The position of firing pointer was a lot of responsibility for a nineteen-year-old kid. I think the reason the officers gave it to me is what they observed in the other sailors. They had a habit of returning to the ship after weekend leave in less than peak condition, whereas I always showed up sober on Monday mornings. I thought it would be good for my career. Apparently I was right.

We were preparing for war, but I still had little reason to believe we'd put our training into practice. Yes, the signs were there for those who were paying attention and astute enough to understand their meaning. An ambitious former artist, Adolf Hitler, ascended to the position of chancellor of Germany in 1933. The following year, Hitler added the title of *Führer* and used his secret police to eliminate scores of his rivals and enemies. Meanwhile, Japan had consolidated its position in

Manchuria after its 1931 invasion and attacked China's Great Wall in Mongolia in 1932. Both Germany and Japan resigned from the League of Nations in 1933.

My crewmates and I on the *West Virginia*, without newspapers or radio, heard only the barest details of these events. Our information was based mostly on gossip rather than facts. We did not anticipate war—and neither did our leaders. After the *West Virginia*, America would not commission another battleship until 1938. We were ill-prepared for the coming storm.

I put away as much of my salary as I could each month, in keeping with my long-term goals. In the meantime, though, I also tried to have as much fun as I could. During my initial training, this meant visiting museums and seeing the sights in places I'd never been before: St. Louis and Chicago. One of the places I visited in Chicago was a speakeasy, an establishment that sold liquor illegally. I believe I got a five-cent Coke for fifty cents. While we were sitting at the bar, a policeman walked in. I was sure I was about to go to jail. But the policeman also sat at the bar and was handed a drink on the house. Selling booze may have been against the law, but apparently the local police made no attempt to enforce it.

After I joined the crew of the *West Virginia*, my travels extended to San Francisco, Seattle, the Hawaiian Islands, the Panama Canal, Haiti, Cuba, and Puerto Rico. In the summer of 1934, I also got my first glimpse of the Big Apple. Since the Navy didn't get to New York often, the city gave us ticker-tape treatment. We marched in a parade up Broadway from the Battery to Central Park, nearly a hundred blocks. I visited museums and took an elevator to the top of what was then the world's tallest structure, the Empire State Building. I also ate hot dogs, sampled the rides, and talked to the girls at Coney Island.

We were given free tickets to the theater and Broadway shows, and admission to any major league baseball park by paying only the twenty-cent tax. I got to watch Babe Ruth and Lou Gehrig suit up for the Cardinals' old nemesis, the Yankees, at Yankee Stadium. Ruth played only a few innings, but watching his performance in warm-up practice—they didn't call it batting practice yet—was better than watching the game. He knocked twenty-five or thirty balls out of the park.

In size and scope, New York City was a long way from Plevna, Missouri. I thoroughly enjoyed it.

I had a different kind of fun one time when I was home on leave. My brother Donald arranged a boxing match, complete with gloves and a ring, between me and the town bully. My opponent didn't last long. When someone asked how I learned to box like that, I said, "Oh, didn't I mention it? We have a boxing league on the *West Virginia*, and I won my weight class."

Back on the ship, I worked to advance the other half of my goals by learning how to beat the system. For example, every Saturday an officer conducted an inspection. The sailor with the neatest uniform got the weekend off. This was no small privilege, since we were granted leave only every other weekend. I decided to buy a new uniform, shoes and all, which I kept in my locker and wore only for inspections. I began winning the inspection competition every Saturday, which meant I got every weekend off. It reached the point where the officer, to save time, walked right over to me when he began his inspection.

I also learned to show up for watches and other work details five minutes earlier than everyone else and to stay five minutes later than everyone else. The officers noticed what I was doing and began giving me the best assignments, which eventually led to faster-than-average promotions.

My naval career was off to a fine start during those first two years. I was "seeing the world," just as I'd hoped. My intention of eventually going to college and law school and into politics remained intact. Everything was going according to plan.

So why was I so miserable?

★3★

SWEET MUSIC

AFTER I JOINED THE NAVY, it didn't take me long to observe that my crewmates were, for the most part, an unhappy bunch. They pretended everything was fine, but I could see that deep down they were dissatisfied with themselves and their lives. The escape for many of them was alcohol.

I was no exception to this general discontent. I was looking for something and had no idea where to find it. Despite the progress of my naval career, I was frustrated. I felt no peace. I couldn't put my finger on what was wrong, but I knew I was deeply unhappy.

I began to imitate the sailors around me, smoking cigarettes and occasionally drinking a bit of wine in an effort to forget about my state of mind. When I went home for leave and my mother learned of my smoking and drinking, she was horrified. I never got drunk, though. That could jeopardize my well-planned future.

Other than the smoking and occasional drinking, I hid my discontent well. As far as the officers and sailors around me were concerned, I was an ambitious seaman second class who was ready to take on the world.

One man who felt I had the potential to make an impact on the world was my division officer, Lieutenant Hilyer Gearing. He said I should be an officer. Lieutenant Gearing asked if I had any political connections, someone who could nominate me for officer training. Since my dad had recently run successfully for a position as a Missouri state representative and was a friend and ally of our US congressman, M. A. Romjue, the answer was yes. But at nineteen, I was past the age limit for applying to the US Naval Academy.

Gearing was persistent: "How about the US Military Academy at West Point?" When we discovered the age limit for entrance was twenty-two, he urged me to apply. It seemed like another opportunity to advance toward my goals, so I agreed.

Gearing took his idea to the ship's executive officer, Commander J. B. Oldendorf (later to be named an admiral). The commander thought it would be a feather in the navy's cap to have a sailor at West Point. He helped me get copies of the entrance examination from the past ten years and appointed the chaplain and two ensigns to tutor me. Gearing, meanwhile, arranged for me to be free from all ship's duties for the next year so I could study. The navy was making every effort to ensure my success.

I wasn't as enthusiastic as Lieutenant Gearing about a new career in the army, but since he believed in and supported me, I was willing to fully commit to preparing for the exam. I had a quiet place to work in the turret and often studied late, even all night. I imagined myself as an army colonel in charge of a brigade of men. A new picture of my future seemed to be coming into focus.

And I could not have been more wrong about it.

Two of my friends aboard the *West Virginia* were a pair of sailors named Lester Spencer and Virgil Hook. Lester was a mess cook. He was nearly six feet tall, a muscular football player from Illinois. Virgil was a Colorado boy, about four inches shorter than Lester and slight by comparison.

What these two had in common was that they were both Christians. What seemed even more unusual to me is that both were interested in *my* spiritual welfare.

My mother had given me a Bible during my first Christmas home from the navy. I found an important use for it—I kept it in my locker and always hid a few bills between its pages. One day a friend asked me to loan him five dollars. I opened my locker, pulled out the Bible, and handed him the money. Lester saw the whole thing.

"That Bible is good for something other than to keep your money in," Lester said. "You should read it."

After a weekend leave a few weeks later, I noticed Lester had a black eye. "If you'd keep out of the bars," I said, "you wouldn't get beat up."

"I didn't get the black eye in a bar," he replied. "I got it playing football. I'm a Christian. I don't go to the bars."

It was the most direct statement of Christian faith I'd ever heard. To my thinking, that made Lester a religious fanatic. But he was such a nice guy that I couldn't help liking him anyway.

I'd grown up going to the Baptist church in Plevna. But for me, as was probably true for most of the folks in Plevna, church was mainly a social enterprise. I believed in God, but there was little depth to my faith. I didn't think much about it and made no effort to further understand or develop it. It was as if I'd run into Jesus at the altar and said, "Nice to have met you. I'll see you in heaven."

In the fall of 1928, when I was fifteen, our family embarked on a ten-thousand-mile journey that lasted seven months and delayed my sophomore year of high school by a year. We traveled as far west as San Bernardino, California, and as far east as DeLand, Florida. While we were in Gulfport, Mississippi, a preacher stopped by the house where we were staying and talked to us Downing children, asking why we hadn't received Jesus Christ as our savior and been baptized. I understood the preacher's message and felt a desire to respond but did not commit my life to Christ.

Lester Spencer's approach to faith was different from anything I'd encountered before. He doggedly pursued God—and he wanted to take me with him on the hunt. I wasn't interested and resisted Lester's efforts.

Finally, though, I gave in. In December 1933, I reluctantly agreed to join Lester and Virgil in spending a day of weekend leave visiting a married couple they knew. The couple's apartment was in San Pedro, a few miles west of the harbor in Long Beach. I'd already heard much from Lester and Virgil about how wonderful these two were. Their names were Dawson and Lila Trotman.

From the buildup my friends had given me about twenty-seven-year-old Dawson, I expected to meet some kind of rugged Superman. Instead, I was introduced to a 120-pound man with a small waist, slender ankles, and a head that seemed too large for his body. Dawson grasped my hand with as firm a grip as his slender arm and bony hand could muster. He introduced himself in a high-pitched voice. I regarded him as an unimpressive civilian, which in my book was strike one against him.

Lila impressed me more. She was four months younger than I, though she seemed older. Noticeably pregnant with their first child, Lila was beautiful, motherly, and hospitable. She seemed the perfect wife and hostess.

The men played volleyball in a nearby park that afternoon; then Dawson took me aside for a private conversation. He opened a Bible often during our talk, but afterward my only memory of our discussion was the word *iniquities*. I'd never heard it before. Apparently he was explaining a passage from the book of Isaiah:

> But he was wounded for our transgressions, he was
> bruised for our iniquities. . . . All we like sheep have
> gone astray; we have turned every one to his own way;
> and the LORD hath laid on him the iniquity of us all.
> ISAIAH 53:5-6

After a delicious chicken dinner, a few more civilians and sailors joined us. Dawson led us in some Christian choruses, none of which was familiar to me. Singing Christian songs was pretty low on my list of pleasures. I felt trapped. It was too far to walk back to the navy landing, and I was not experienced enough in the ways of the world to call a taxi.

After a few rafter-shaking songs, there was a knock on the door. The couple from the apartment below asked us to stop making noise or they would call the police. Dawson chose to exercise his First Amendment right, and the singing continued. The next knock at the door proved to be two burly policemen. They warned us to honor the complaint, or we'd all be arrested.

I was proud of my impeccable conduct record in the navy and resented the possibility of it being compromised by a trip to jail. I also resented my well-meaning Christian friends. I was ready to leave.

The singing stopped. Dawson gave a Bible talk, which I tuned out completely. I was preoccupied with thinking of a way out of there. The Trotmans had a couch and some cushions for overnight guests and invited me to spend the night. I firmly refused and insisted I be taken to the navy landing. My shipmates reminded me that the last boat to the ship had already left at ten o'clock. I didn't care. I was taken back to the landing and spent the night on a hard wooden bench. I got very little sleep but was happy to have escaped that spiritual prison.

My escape turned out to be short-lived.

Another of my navy friends was a stocky six-footer from Appleton, Wisconsin. Ed Goodrick and I met initially as recruits in the drag company back at Great Lakes. We played a number of chess matches during those first weeks before our intensive training began. Ed always won. He was an intellectual and an atheist. He had an ego and could be arrogant at times, but I enjoyed his company.

Ed was on the navy swim team and later became an All-Navy swim champion. One of his teammates, Gurney Harris, was a Christian in Dawson Trotman's circle. Gurney soon went to work on Goodrick.

Ed was as unimpressed with Dawson as I was and perhaps even more resistant to the faith. Yet for some reason he kept joining Gurney and others on weekend visits with the Trotmans. By this time they had moved from San Pedro to a house half a block from the ocean in Long Beach.

One day on the ship in March 1934, Ed approached me with what he considered exciting news—at the Trotman home, he'd "welcomed the Lord Jesus into my life."

I was surprised. I had great respect for Ed. He had a knack for figuring things out. There had to be strong evidence for him to change from an atheist to a Christian. Over the following days and weeks, I observed more changes in Ed—his ego and arrogance disappeared and were replaced by an attitude of humility. He also seemed strangely concerned about my well-being.

Lester, Virgil, Ed, and others kept me abreast of their spiritual advances. They invited me numerous times to again accompany them on visits to the Trotman lair. I appreciated their interest but considered it a distraction. "Ed," I said at one point, "you know if it were not for studying for my entrance exam at West Point, I would be right with you guys." I remained dedicated to my reading.

One day that summer, however, I wore down and agreed to join them. I was ready for a break from the books. It helped that the Trotmans' new home was within walking distance of the navy landing, so I knew I had an escape route.

The meeting centered on a guest speaker, Oscar Zimmerman, who had a ministry to merchant seamen. By this time Lila had given birth to a son, Bruce, who was already at the crawling stage. During the message, Bruce pulled himself up to a window sill, retrieved an object, and put it in his mouth. The object filled his little mouth and he began to discharge noticeable amounts of saliva. One of the sailors picked him up and handed him to Dawson, who reached into Bruce's mouth and produced a double-edged razor blade. There was not even a trace of blood in Bruce's mouth.

I was astonished. Mr. Zimmerman had paused his presentation, so Dawson stood and said, "Let's thank the Lord for protecting Bruce." He led us in a prayer, then turned the meeting back over to the speaker.

As I headed back to the ship, I considered what had happened. The message seemed loud and clear: God was in that home and had a special interest in the family he'd commissioned to occupy it for him. I'd been standing on holy ground.

It gave me much to think about.

It was a warm summer day in 1934. I sat with six other men around long tables. I was the only one dressed in navy whites.

The large room was almost luxurious, with leather furniture, carpet on the floor, and paintings on the walls. I was in the officers' club on the army base at Fort Lewis, Washington. After a year of diligent study, the time had come for me to take the West Point entrance exam.

It quickly turned into a disaster. Though I was very familiar with the first two subjects, history and math, I couldn't concentrate. I fiddled with my pen and stared at the papers in front of me. Then I panicked. The harder I tried to concentrate, the more confused I got.

The papers I handed in before the lunch break were practically blank.

I didn't understand what had happened to me. I'd never had test anxiety before. At lunchtime, I regrouped, and when I returned to the exam room for the afternoon, I was in a better frame of mind. I breezed through the final four subjects and knew I'd scored high marks. But there was no doubt that I'd blown the first two sections.

After all the work I'd put in and everything others had done to help me, I'd failed the exam and let everyone down. This was as low as I'd ever been. That night in Tacoma, I walked the streets near the waterfront and brooded about my failure. The next day I would have to tell everyone what had happened and resume navy responsibilities.

I spotted a hotel across a busy street. As I crossed, I thought seriously about throwing myself in front of a passing car. Life no longer seemed worth living.

I still couldn't understand what had happened to me during the first part of the test. Only later did I consider that spiritual intervention may have had something to do with my inexplicable confusion that morning.

I returned to the *West Virginia* and resumed my normal duties, more unhappy with myself and my life than ever. Soon after, I was assigned to a work detail along with my friend Virgil Hook. We got up at 3:30 a.m., ate baked beans and cornbread for breakfast, and were boated to a provision ship to hand-carry frozen beef from its cargo hold to our battleship. We had to move a three months' supply for fifteen hundred men, so it was a lot of beef.

As I stood in the dark, refrigerated chamber and passed off load after load of frozen animal flesh, my mood dropped further. This was not the glamorous existence I'd expected to find in the navy. I was cold and miserable.

Virgil had a different response. He had a smile on his face and was humming tunes, having the time of his life.

In that forlorn setting, I came to a significant conclusion. Any inward joy I had experienced up to that point in my life was the result of outward favorable circumstances. For instance, I sometimes spent weekends with a group of Hollywood performers. This was in the days of live, nationwide radio entertainment. I had a friend who sang on one of the shows and introduced me to other entertainers. When I was around this crowd, I felt upbeat and important. But when I was stuck moving cold beef for hours at a time, I felt unhappy and insignificant. Unfavorable outward circumstances left me feeling bad on the inside.

Yet here was Virgil Hook, unmoved by circumstances, a man who smiled even in the cold and dark. He was a Christian. He had an inner resource that circumstances couldn't touch.

I wanted his kind of happiness. I needed that resource too.

After a year of preparation for the West Point exam, I was already in the habit of studying. I got rid of all my books except for a volume of Shakespeare and a Bible. I set out to read the entire Bible and discover what it was all about.

As I read at my workbench in the turret, the first verse that made an impression on me was, "He that hath ears to hear, let him hear" (Matthew 11:15). I realized there was something unknown to me that I was supposed to hear.

Eventually I came to another passage that seemed to demand my attention:

That if thou shalt confess with thy mouth the Lord Jesus, and shalt believe in thine heart that God hath raised him from the dead, thou shalt be saved.

For with the heart man believeth unto righteousness; and with the mouth confession is made unto salvation.

ROMANS 10:9-10

I highlighted the passage and put the Bible on my shelf. This was the message I was supposed to hear. Until I was ready to follow its instructions, my spiritual journey was on hold.

In the early months of 1935, the *West Virginia* was docked in Bremerton, Washington, for a routine overhaul. The "Dawsonites," as Ed and the others sometimes referred to themselves, had been put in charge of a Sunday-evening service at a Bremerton church. They invited me to join them, and I accepted.

My friends taught the hundred or so members of the

45

Bremerton congregation a new worship song and led them in singing. Then, one by one, they went up to the front of the church and shared the story of how each came to know Jesus Christ. Ed sat on a bench in the row just ahead of me. As this part of the service began, he leaned back and said, "Jim, would you like to give a testimony?"

"No," I whispered. "I really don't believe in that stuff."

But as I sat on that bench and listened to the others speak, the words of the passage from Romans began occupying my heart and mind. It was a challenge, I realized. God was promising that if I would publicly identify with Christ as Lord, my soul would be saved.

I wanted assurance that I would spend eternity in heaven. This seemed the sure way to get it. I nudged Ed's shoulder. "I'll do it," I said. "Call on me."

A few minutes later, I stood in front of the congregation and tried to mix humor and my navy experience in my brief talk. I said that life before knowing Christ was like going to sea in a sieve, but that after one becomes a Christian, he's not sinking anymore. It wasn't much of a message. The guys later told me it was one of the most unimpressive statements of faith they'd ever heard. But I felt I'd done what God wanted me to do.

Back on the ship that night, I was the happiest I'd ever been. This was the feeling of fulfillment I'd been searching for.

In the morning, I woke up with a song in my heart. I went to work in turret two, in a private space like an underground tunnel, chipping paint with a pneumatic hammer. It was noisy, dusty, and dark, but I didn't even notice. I felt a joy and peace I'd never known before.

All of a sudden, though, those feelings disappeared, replaced by the old misery and emptiness. I wanted the joy and peace back.

I shut off the air hammer and thought. I realized that God had given me a glimpse of a heavenly gift. To keep it, I would have to follow him.

I had one last reservation. I feared that if I committed myself to Christ, he might want me to be a missionary or preacher. I didn't want to do that. But if the navy had taught me anything, it was that obedience cannot be halfhearted. It must be 100 percent. I also finally understood that God would more than compensate for any seeming sacrifice I might make.

Standing alone in the bowels of turret two, I bowed my head. It was 7:45 a.m. on April 8, 1935. "Lord," I prayed, "whatever it means to give my life to you, I want to do that. I'm going to give my life to you even if it means being a missionary or preacher. No reservations. I'm yours now."

I resumed my work. Once again, the sound of the air hammer was sweet music—the joy and peace had returned. They have been with me ever since.

The road to heavenly fulfillment would not always be smooth. The Sunday after my life-changing prayer was Palm Sunday. I felt I should be in church worshiping, but I had already purchased a ticket to attend the finals of the US national championship and Olympic team tryouts for downhill and slalom skiing, to be held on Washington's Mount Rainier. I decided to go to the ski event.

On the bus to Mount Rainier, I recognized a yeoman from

the *West Virginia*. He wasn't a friend, but I knew his name, so I sat with him. At each stop on the way, we got off the bus to have a beer or smoke cigarettes. As we neared our destination, I sensed the Lord prompting me to talk with this man about Jesus. But I didn't do it. I felt I'd compromised my credibility by smoking and drinking with him. I decided to wait until we got back to the ship to talk with him about my newfound faith.

After the ski event, we parted ways at the bus station. I took a late-afternoon bus to my hotel. Two days later, my morning newspaper brought shocking news: A man had committed suicide by jumping out of a third-floor window at the same hotel where I'd been staying.

It was my bus companion.

I was devastated. I'd had no idea my shipmate was despondent or considering taking his life. But God had known. He had put this man and me together. I'd failed him. And I'd failed the Lord.

My fledgling faith took on a new urgency. I had been granted salvation and a peace and joy that would sustain me into eternity, but I'd missed an opportunity to pass on these gifts to someone who had desperately needed them.

I resolved to make sure it never happened again.

★4★

INSIDE MAN

AT THE SAME TIME that I was committing myself to the tenets of the Christian faith, much of the rest of the world was steadily moving away from them. Nationalism, militarism, and expansionism were increasingly the favored guiding principles for global leaders—particularly in Germany and Japan.

Two months after my conversion to Christianity aboard the *West Virginia*, the Germans signed an agreement with Britain allowing them to build their navy up to 35 percent of the tonnage of the British Royal Navy. This agreement effectively nullified the Treaty of Versailles, the agreement between Germany and the Allied Forces that ended World War I. The English, believing that they were improving global security by confining Adolf Hitler's ambitions, negotiated the new agreement without consulting their Allied partners, France and Italy. The controversial decision has been acknowledged by history as a precursor to Britain's ill-fated policy of appeasement toward Hitler and the resurgence of Germany as a military power.

I often tell people that *weakness invites aggression.* So does appeasement. Treaties that attempt to appease aggression rather than confront it create a false sense of security: They are generally unenforceable, and often the signers have no intention of carrying out provisions of enforcement. Treaties are meant to provide for our national security, but when negotiated from weakness, they often compromise it.

On September 15, 1935, at a meeting of the German parliament in Nuremberg, Hitler announced a law that effectively stripped German Jews of their citizenship and other rights. The Law for the Protection of German Blood and German Honor forbade the marriage of Jews and non-Jews, nullifying such marriages even in foreign nations. It also made extramarital sexual relations between Jews and non-Jews illegal. Jews were forbidden from employing female Germans under the age of forty-five in their homes and were prohibited from displaying the swastika, the symbol of the Nazi Party that had become the new national flag.

As bad as the new law was for German Jews, the worst was yet to come.

In February 1936, Germany hosted the Winter Olympics in Garmisch-Partenkirchen. Some of the same athletes I'd watched perform on Mount Rainier would compete there. Less than a month later, on March 7, thirty thousand German troops marched into the demilitarized Rhineland, in open defiance of the Treaty of Versailles.

Hitler was gambling that the world was not ready for war. He later described the next forty-eight hours as the tensest of his life.

Hitler's instincts were correct. Germany's aggressive action went unchallenged. World leaders wanted peace so badly that they were willing to be fooled by Hitler's supposedly benign intentions. Joseph Goebbels, Hitler's minister of propaganda, wrote in his diary, "The Fuehrer is immensely happy. . . . England remains passive. France won't act alone. Italy is disappointed and America is uninterested."

The charade continued a few months later in Berlin with the summer Olympic Games. Germany made its case for racial supremacy by winning eighty-nine medals—the most of any country. The hosts also impressed their guests from around the globe with a clean and efficient city. Even the taxi drivers and garbage collectors wore new uniforms.

The Japanese, meanwhile, also were positioning themselves for aggressive action. In the final days of 1934, they renounced naval treaties with the United States and the United Kingdom. In February 1936, a failed coup d'état allowed the military to exert even more control over the civilian government. That summer, Japan entered into negotiations with Germany over an agreement that would bind each in a partnership if either was attacked by the Soviet Union. The two nations would sign the pact by the end of the year.

The differences between the Christian faith I had just adopted and the attitudes toward religion of the governing leaders of these two nations were stark. Jesus' teaching emphasized themes of love ("For God so loved the world, that he gave his only begotten Son, that whosoever believeth in him should not perish, but have everlasting life"—John 3:16), equality ("There is neither Jew nor Greek, there is neither bond nor free, there is neither male nor female: for ye are all one in Christ Jesus"—Galatians 3:28), and humility ("So the last shall be first, and the first last"—Matthew 20:16). Hitler, meanwhile, believed in German racial purity, an Aryan master race destined to rule the world. The ideal Aryan in Hitler's eyes was tall, blond, and blue-eyed. One can only imagine what he thought during the 1936 Summer Olympics when America's Jesse Owens—continuously referred to by German broadcasters and journalists as "the Negro Owens"—won four gold medals, the most for an individual at the games.

Especially during his early years in power, Hitler often made pro-Christian or pro-church statements. But that was only to further his plan to eventually use the church to promote Nazi ideology. In truth, he had no use for the Christian faith. As he said more than once to close associates, "It's been our misfortune to have the wrong religion. Why didn't we have the religion of the Japanese, who regard sacrifice for the Fatherland as the highest good? The Mohammedan religion too would have been much more compatible to us than Christianity. Why did it have to be Christianity with its meekness and flabbiness?"

Japan's leader was the Emperor Hirohito, who was said to have divine power. The Shinto religion held that the Japanese imperial family was the offspring of the sun goddess Amaterasu. The origins of Japan's twentieth-century ambitions could be traced back 2,500 years to the sun goddess, who reportedly envisioned a future island empire and a world that was subject to her descendants.

By 1935, Japan was religiously syncretistic, its people practicing a mixture of Shinto and Buddhism. The government's propaganda ministers, however, tied the fulfillment of one's religious duty with the nation's political and military goals, summarized by the phrase "the Imperial Way." As one Japanese general put it two years after the invasion of Manchuria, "Every single bullet must be charged with the Imperial Way, and the end of every bayonet must have National Virtue burnt into it." Much like Hitler, government officials framed the upcoming conflict as Japanese purity versus impurity. Western nations such as the United States, they said, were corrupt, morally degenerate, and materialistic. Japanese children in the military-run school system were drilled for combat and taught that it was their divinely mandated destiny to rule over the rest of the world's inferior and impure races.

I was not aware of all this at the time of my 1935 spiritual conversion. In fact, my shipmates and I were under the influence of a different brand of propaganda. Though we suspected that the Germans might one day cause some serious trouble, we were told and believed that the Japanese didn't see well and couldn't shoot straight, and that everything they made was junk. We figured if we ever did find ourselves in a war with the Japanese, we'd wipe them out in three months.

A few days after my prayer in turret two, Ed Goodrick and another Christian friend, John Dedrick, met with me to follow up on my decision and guide my fledgling spiritual journey. They began by giving me what they called the Wheel

Illustration, a concept that had been created by Dawson Trotman. Christ was represented as the hub of the wheel. The role of a Christian was represented by four spokes: the Word (Bible study), Prayer, Witnessing (telling others about Jesus), and Living the (Christian) Life.

As they were explaining the illustration to me, another sailor who worked with me heard our conversation and became curious. So Dedrick began explaining the gospel to him. I was amazed at the skill and familiarity with which Dedrick used Bible passages to answer the man's every question and objection. After seeing this, I decided I needed to learn more Scripture. I heard about a 108-verse Scripture memory course and got a list of the verses. I memorized ten a day until I learned them all.

Despite my West Point failure, my benefactor, Lieutenant Gearing, was still eager to help me in my career. Eager, that is, until I told him about my decision to give my life to Christ. "Oh, no!" was his response. He followed this by writing me a long note about what a great mistake I was making. My father had a similar reaction—as a lifelong Baptist, he considered anything outside our church denomination a cult. But I was undeterred. I'd seen the difference that Jesus made in others, and I felt it in myself. I was all-in. Furthermore, I was now ready to join the band of sailors under the influence of the small but enthusiastic man from Long Beach, Dawson Trotman.

Dawson had begun his navy ministry two years earlier with Lester Spencer. By this time he had recruited five men to join him in his quest to tell the world about Jesus. I was number six. The group needed a name. Dawson had been spending time with a sailor who was studying celestial navigation, and when he saw the man's chart and compass, it occurred to Dawson that we are all engaged in a kind of spiritual navigation. We became, officially, The Navigators.

My allegiance was sealed on one of my off days back in Long Beach. Dawson had invited me to accompany him on his appointments. He picked me up at the navy landing, but instead of taking me to his home, he pulled his 1932 Packard into the nearest parking place. Still sitting behind the wheel, he opened his Bible and said with excitement, "I have something to show you." He put the Bible in front of me and read Isaiah 58:12: "And they that shall be of thee shall build the old waste places: thou shalt raise up the foundations of many generations; and thou shalt be called, The repairer of the breach, The restorer of paths to dwell in."

"I am scared to death," Dawson confided, "but I know God has told me he is going to do this through me." He had been called to raise and fortify the spiritual foundations of many generations. This was no small mission. Like Hitler and Hirohito, but in a very different manner and with a very different goal, Dawson felt his destiny was to change the world.

Sitting in the Packard with Dawson that day, I resolved that I would throw my life in with him. I saw that he was involved in the major leagues of life both here and hereafter, and I wanted to be included.

The Long Beach ministry was built around a Friday-night meeting in the Trotman living room and a Saturday recreational afternoon followed by another meeting that night. Between eighteen and twenty-five people attended each time, most of them new Christians brought to the home by more mature believers.

By summer 1935, four of Dawson's original Navigators had been discharged from the navy. Only Ed Goodrick and I remained on the *West Virginia*. Ed took over the mantle of leadership for a brief time, then deferred to me, apparently feeling I'd do a better job. It was both exciting and a daunting duty for someone who'd been a practicing Christian for only three months and was leader by default.

The *West Virginia* spent at least half of its time at sea in training maneuvers and made stops in many ports. We were without Dawson's leadership during those times and had to provide our own. Yet our battleship was a perfect environment for spreading God's message. A sailor's workday ended at 3:30 p.m., followed by two hours for leisure and taking care of personal necessities like laundry. The evening meal was finished by 6:00. Those men not on watch had an hour and a half of free time until the nightly movie was shown on the fantail of the ship, weather and training maneuvers permitting.

Those ninety minutes after dinner were a prime opportunity for us to fan out throughout the ship, connect with those we'd talked with and prayed for previously, and make new contacts. Our team met for prayer for fifteen minutes before every meal. When the movie started at 7:30 each evening, we met for another two-and-a-half hours. During these gatherings, we studied the Bible and prayed for each other and our shipmates. We believed the best example we could give of Christ's presence in our lives was to be the best in our profession, so we prayed to attain that goal. On Tuesday nights, we held an evangelistic study for the crew that was announced over the ship's loudspeaker. Christians who wanted to attend had to bring at least one non-Christian or prove they had spent at least an hour trying to get someone to come.

The *West Virginia* became a floating seminary. It was fertile ground. Many of our non-Christian shipmates knew, at least subconsciously, that there was more to life than serving in the navy and carousing on weekend leaves. Our job was to introduce them to a better and eternal way of life.

★   ★   ★

My rank in 1935 was seaman second class. I'd been aboard the *West Virginia* for two years. I intended to improve my position.

The navy held competitive examinations for the scarce advancements available on each ship. For the first time, I was eligible for the exam. I studied books on navy regulations, general military knowledge, and detailed questions about the specialty I was pursuing: gunner's mate.

The exam took longer than anticipated, and no one was finished by noon "chow time." When an officer announced that the exam would be completed after a lunch break, we all did the same thing—we made note of the questions we didn't know the answers to, and instead of eating lunch, we looked up the answers. Not surprisingly, there were some pretty high scores.

My conscience bothered me, however. Now that I was a Christian, I wasn't comfortable with my behavior. Before I turned in the exam, I placed a checkmark beside the questions I'd researched the answers to and wrote an explanation of what I'd done.

Confessing to my "crime" did not hurt my career—it helped.

The examining officer put my name near the top of the promotion list. I was advanced to seaman first class at a salary of $54 a month.

I did nearly derail my career, however. I had a pre-breakfast routine of phoning the engineering office at 5:30 a.m. and requesting they turn on electrical power for turret two, so that we could lower and scrub the gun barrels and polish the brass-decorated plugs that sealed the muzzles of the guns. One morning, not long after the exam, I dialed the number as usual. Instead of the prompt "Log Room" answer I expected, the phone rang about a dozen times. Finally, someone picked up and said in a gruff voice, "Hello."

I requested power for turret two.

The gruff voice responded, "This is the captain. Watch those numbers when you dial them." He slammed down the receiver.

Apparently I'd dialed a wrong number by accident—the captain's unpublished cabin number. If the captain tried to track down his early-morning tormenter, however, he never succeeded. I was soon promoted to gunner's mate third class.

In September 1936, I had to make a decision. My two-year navy enlistment was about to expire. At this point I had no intention of making a career of the navy. In the back of my mind, I still had the idea of a career in politics. My immediate choice was to either follow my Christian associates into civilian life and enroll in college, or to reenlist for another two years.

As I prayed and sought the counsel of Dawson Trotman and others, I felt God give me a clear answer. The future of The Navigators seemed to depend on the presence of an inside man in the navy. I was willing to be that man. I would stay in the navy until the Lord indicated otherwise. I wrote a letter to Dawson announcing my decision; he took the stamp off the envelope and pasted it in his Bible with a note about its significance.

Two years later, when my next enlistment period ended, nothing had changed in the arrangement between the Lord and me. So I signed up for another four years. My navy career would last until at least 1942.

A gunner's mate is part of a team responsible for maintenance, battle readiness, and operation of the guns in each turret. Since exposure to seawater causes rust, we had to constantly oil, polish, and paint the guns and turret. To actually fire a gun, we jammed a projectile into the barrel, slid powder behind the projectile, closed the breech, inserted a firing cartridge, and pulled the trigger.

Some of my other duties aboard the ship included gun pointer and captain, motor whaleboat crewman, and assistant to the master-at-arms. These responsibilities gave me wide exposure to several officers. My relationships with them, as well as my civilian experience with the Plevna post office, came in handy when the assistant navy mail clerk was assigned to new duty. I was appointed to take his place.

In 1937, I became the *West Virginia*'s navy mail clerk, or postmaster. Military leaders have concluded that mail is more important to fighting men than food. Because of this, we used ship's aircraft to make mail runs once or twice a week when we were within two to three hundred miles of land. I received a 50 percent increase in pay by flying four hours per month, since flying was technically considered hazardous duty. Just as big a bonus was having a private office. I kept my cot and bedding inside the office and was able to determine my own sleeping hours.

Thanks to my new duties, all of the officers and men knew me by sight and name. I knew most of their names, too, as well as the names of their wives and girlfriends. At one time we had five James Smiths on board—it took some effort to keep them straight.

The men treated me much as they would a weather forecaster. When my shipmates received letters containing good news, they gave me the credit. When they got no mail or bad news, I got the blame.

Every payday, most of the men sent money to family members. On the fifth and twentieth of each month, my assistant and I wrote about $10,000 in money orders. As postmaster, I was also bonded and responsible for funds collected when crew members sent telegrams though the ship's radio system. I turned the cash over to the ship's disbursing officer at the end of each day.

I took my postmaster duties seriously and made sure to keep good accounts of the money I handled. Apparently a few of my colleagues on other ships were less than honest when it came to finances and had a bad reputation. One rumor I heard was that the naval prison on Mare Island, California, held a baseball series each year. The teams of prisoners were divided between former commissary stewards and mail clerks. Supposedly, they had more than enough players to fill out each squad.

Another important bonus to my position as postmaster was that contact with the entire crew allowed me to develop deeper relationships with them. To show my interest in the men, I tried to serve beyond the call of duty. For example, I devised a system that eliminated the long lines and waits for crewmen who wanted to send a money order on payday. They could apply and pay for the money order fee in advance, and I would write up their order the night before, so when they arrived they just had to present a number. It was a small thing that softened some of their hearts. It seemed that God knew just how to use me for his purposes.

I was about to discover that he had another surprise waiting for me.

★5★

THEN THERE WAS MORENA

DURING MY ELEVEN YEARS OF SCHOOLING in Plevna and my final year at Novelty High, the number of girls and of boys was about equal. Having been in school together for three-fourths of our lifetimes, we had formed opinions of each other's strengths and weaknesses—mostly the latter. There was little if any romantic interest. The girls we met from other schools in the county looked more interesting, but since the roads were drivable for only part of the year, we didn't have the means to follow through. Our romantic impulses were not strong enough motivation for a four- to six-hour horseback ride.

By the time I joined the navy, I'd had less than a half dozen dates in my life. One of the girls in my class, Eldora Fite, was sharp academically, and we were good friends. But when I left

Plevna for my training in Great Lakes, I broke no young maidens' hearts and had no one outside of my family to write to.

After I gave my life to Christ, I was still largely inexperienced in affairs of the heart. This was not due to lack of interest but lack of opportunity. I naturally hoped to find a similarly devoted Christian girl, and I met plenty during shore team meetings with young people's groups. But we navy Navigators had a strict rule—no giving out our names and addresses, no matter how badly a girl might want a "follow-up" meeting.

My fortunes finally began to change in October 1939. Dawson had invited a mixed quartet from the Bible Institute of Los Angeles (now Biola University) to sing for us less talented Christians at one of our Saturday-night meetings at the Trotman home. One member of the quartet was a senior alto named Morena Holmes.

A few days later, I was at Dawson's Los Angeles office when Morena walked in. She led the Bible clubs for the Navigator high school girls and was there to consult with Dawson. He introduced us.

From that first meeting, I still remember Morena's red hair, brown leather shoes, and bright smile. After she left, I asked Dawson about her. Morena was from Arkansas and lived month to month—she would get through four years of college without ever having any guaranteed income. She made up for her lack of funds with a strong faith. Dawson described her as a gifted spiritual person. I decided I wanted to get to know her better.

A few weeks later, The Navigators held a weekend conference at Pacific Palisades, California. Morena was there to sing.

During one of the meals I spotted a vacant chair next to her, which I promptly occupied.

Morena and I had only a brief conversation about the conference, nothing personal. Nevertheless, my actions did not go unnoticed by my friends, who began to snicker, "Downing's got a girl."

When Dawson smelled romance blooming, he followed it through with the persistence of a bloodhound on the trail. He and Lila took special measures to see that I accompanied them to Morena's graduation from the Bible institute in June 1940. She was the graduating class women's speaker and wore a long, beautiful white dress. Her talk wowed the audience, me included.

After the ceremony, Morena was surrounded by friends and admirers. I had prayed that if the Lord wanted us to get better acquainted, I would have the opportunity to speak to her at graduation. Judging from the size of the mob around her, however, it appeared my prayer wouldn't be answered the way I'd hoped.

Suddenly, miraculously, the circle of admirers and well-wishers parted like the Red Sea. Morena stood alone, no one within twenty-five feet of her.

I hurried over and asked about her immediate plans. She was going to spend the summer with a child-evangelism team in Arkansas and move into the Trotmans' Long Beach home in the fall. I told her I was going back to sea soon—we were stationed now at Pearl Harbor in Hawaii. I said I would pray for her.

After Morena left for the summer, Dawson gave me a handwritten note that included these words:

> Personally I regard M. H. as one of the three or
> four most outstanding women I have known in the
> years of my Christian life (some fourteen). When
> I told her you were #1 Navigator—boy, she smiled
> beautiful 'n' everything.

Morena Holmes had certainly made an impression on me, but for now I had to put aside any thoughts of a potential romance. The female that demanded most of my attention was still a battleship named the *West Virginia*.

That summer, the *West Virginia* left Long Beach for the Southwest Pacific Ocean as part of the US Pacific Fleet. During the previous three years, looming clouds had been threatening to spoil America's blue skies. In 1937, Japan had invaded China, a longtime US ally. In late 1937, the Japanese attacked an American gunboat on the Yangtze River in China, straining relations with the United States but otherwise prompting little response.

The next year, the Germans annexed Austria and persuaded the United Kingdom, France, and Italy to allow them to take over the Sudetenland area of Czechoslovakia, another vain attempt at appeasing Hitler. By March 1939, Germany occupied the rest of Czechoslovakia. The American people remained largely isolationist and unmoved by the rest of the world's problems—a posture that would soon prove shortsighted and that certainly fell short of the Christian ideal of loving your neighbor and acting on behalf of justice.

When Hitler's troops invaded Poland in September 1939, the other nations of Europe could close their eyes no longer. England, France, and other allies declared war on Germany. Russia, at that time a German ally, annexed part of Poland and invaded Finland. By May 1940, Germany's reach extended to France, Belgium, Luxembourg, and the Netherlands. Closer to home in the Pacific, Japan expanded its incursion into China and threatened the US territories Hawaii, Wake, Guam, and Midway, as well as the commonwealth of the Philippines.

The result of the world's policies of appeasement and isolationism was proving to be catastrophic. It will always be so against the likes of dictators and tyrants. We Americans and many other nations were naive and unprepared for the onslaught launched by Hitler and Hirohito. We must always remain strong, courageous, and vigilant—innocent as doves, yes, but wise as serpents—if we expect to keep the wolves at bay.

In addition to training, our preparations on the *West Virginia* included a traditional navy ceremony for crossing the equator. Those of us who had yet to cross, known as "pollywogs," had to pass an initiation to be considered "shellbacks" and members of Neptune's kingdom. The night before our crossing, I and others were put in makeshift stocks. I was made to gargle an evil-tasting liquid, and then I was blindfolded and my stomach was sterilized with salt water, to prepare me for my "operation." A knife was swiped across my skin, charged with electricity so that it felt like a deep cut. The blindfolds came off, and our hands and feet were bound. A red-paint-covered rubber blade was dropped on our necks so we could fully appreciate the effect of a guillotine. Finally, my fellow initiates and I were again blindfolded and instructed to lie flat on a board. I was lifted high into the air, and then thrown into the sea. At least, that's what it felt like. Only after the blindfolds came off did I realize that we'd been tossed into a canvas-enclosed pool of seawater.

I'm not certain how much the ceremony prepared us for battle, but it did boost morale. Since each of us had suffered the same fate, we felt a closer bond than ever before. In the fight to come, we would need every edge we could get.

Following the crossing, I retreated to the solitude of the post office. During a time of prayer, I asked the Lord if there was anything he wanted me to do that I hadn't done.

It was almost as if I heard an audible voice: "How about Morena?"

That wasn't what I expected. But I felt I would be disobedient if I didn't respond. So I wrote Morena a letter. In it, I said I wondered if the Lord might want our lives linked together in ministry, and that I looked forward to getting to know her better the next time we met.

Instead of mailing the letter, I put it in my desk drawer. Even with the Lord's prompting, I wasn't ready to reveal my thoughts just yet. I might have transformed from a pollywog to a shellback, but crossing the line that protected Morena's heart felt like much more dangerous waters.

Though the *West Virginia* was now stationed at Pearl Harbor, we stopped in Long Beach in fall 1940 for a few weeks. Morena had moved into the Trotman home, and I found myself spending my spare time there. Because the home was small and several college girls lived there, Morena had no separate room and slept on the living-room sofa. She couldn't turn in for the night until all the guests had left, which was often late.

Morena told me that she'd been praying for me during the summer. One of my own prayers had been that my future wife would pray for me at least six months before our marriage. So I was encouraged by this news.

About a year before, I'd purchased a 1937 Chevrolet in Seattle and left it with the Trotmans so the team would have a way to get around. Now I put the Chevrolet to use for another purpose. I needed to drive to San Pedro to pick up some materials for a friend, so I invited Morena to come along. She had dishwashing duty at the house and wasn't free, but with lightning speed the Trotmans found a replacement.

The letter I'd written weeks before and neglected to mail was in my pocket. I was ready to cross that line.

We reached our destination in San Pedro. Before I got out of the car, I handed Morena the letter and said as casually as I could, "This is a letter I wrote to you but hadn't mailed yet." When I returned she was reading a magazine, matching my casualness.

On the drive back to Long Beach, Morena didn't have much to say. It wasn't until I parked the car outside the home that we finally talked about the letter. Perhaps understandably, she'd interpreted my words as a marriage proposal. In the back of my mind, I knew this was the direction I eventually wanted to go, but I was shocked by the speed at which we were getting there.

"That's—that's not what I meant," I said.

It took a few attempts to sort out our communication and

for me to retract my unintended proposal. My awkwardness probably would have been irreparable except for the fact that Morena had inside information from the Lord—she'd told her mother that summer that I was the man she would marry.

Dawson and Lila tried to get our relationship back in the fast lane. They told me that Morena needed background information on sailors she'd be writing about as editor of the *Navigators Log* publication. Since I knew the men better than anyone, they said, I should give her a briefing. Morena and I sat down in the bedroom Dawson had turned into an office and began to leaf through some files. Dawson, Lila, and other guests retired to the living room to plot and pray. I heard a few giggles coming from their direction.

After a few minutes of pretending to carry out our artificial assignment, I saw through this not-too-subtle setup. I loved being with Morena, but this felt too arranged, so I suggested we join the others in the living room. I will never forget the surprised and disappointed looks on their faces as we emerged after such a brief tryst.

The next day, Dawson pulled me aside to apply more pressure. "Listen, Morena isn't the kind of girl who will wait around. If you don't make a move, someone else will."

I knew Dawson's matchmaking was well intentioned, but I did not want to be pushed into action. "If someone else can get her," I said, "that is all the proof I need that God doesn't intend her for me."

Despite my resistance, however, I could not deny my attraction to Morena or my hope that our futures would merge. I again employed the Chevrolet and took her on several rides in the area. On one of the last days of 1940, a beautiful sunny California afternoon, we sat alone on a bench overlooking the ocean. We watched the tide come in, smelled the seashells on the beach, and felt a gentle ocean breeze wash over us.

The mystery and chemistry of what the wise man in the Bible's book of Proverbs described as "the way of a man with a maid" overcame me. I knew that I wanted to spend the rest of my life with this girl. In fact, the feeling in my heart was so strong that it spilled over into my stomach. I felt ill and told Morena so.

"I know what's the matter," she said. "You're sick with love." Always the good Bible student, she had diagnosed my problem with a passage from Song of Solomon.

I knew it was time. I took Morena's hands in mine. "When we talked before about our lives being linked together," I said, "I didn't mean marriage. But now I do. Will you marry me?"

Morena's response was an enthusiastic "Gladly!" We sealed the arrangement with a kiss.

On New Year's Eve, I announced our engagement to a group of mostly sailors at the Trotmans' new home in Hollywood. We Navigators never did anything without the support of Scripture, so my choice to accompany the announcement was Job 3:25: "For the thing which I greatly feared is come upon me, and that which I was afraid of is come unto me."

Morena didn't find it particularly spiritual or romantic.

Soon after, I set sail on the *West Virginia*. The ship was due for a three-month overhaul in Bremerton. Before I left, we bought a marriage license in California and planned to marry as soon as the ship returned to Long Beach. But deteriorating relations with Japan disrupted our plans.

The United States was implementing increasingly strict limits on exports of war-related material to the Japanese. In September, Japan signed the Tripartite Pact, which formally established the Axis triangle of Germany, Italy, and Japan. In response to these and other events, the navy kept the *West Virginia* operational. Our return to the mainland was deferred indefinitely; Pearl Harbor would once again be our base of operations.

Morena's prolonged stay with the Trotmans finally ended when Dawson emptied their cash jar and provided the forty dollars needed for a one-way ticket to Honolulu aboard the luxury liner *Matsonia*. I was at sea when Morena arrived, so Harold and Belva DeGroff greeted her with a traditional lei ceremony. They invited Morena to stay at their home in the Kalihi Valley. We arranged to be married at our favorite conference center in the Kokokahi area on the north side of Oahu.

On the afternoon of July 10, 1941, the day before the wedding, I picked up our marriage license at the Honolulu city clerk's office. The clerk asked where we were going to be married. When I told her Kokokahi, she said, "This license is not good there. It is only good in the judicial district of the city of Honolulu."

I panicked. There was a three-day waiting period before the license we needed was valid. The clerk let me stew for a few minutes, then said, "This happens often. You will have to have two weddings."

She showed me a map. The closest location to Kokokahi where we could use the license was the Pali, a mountain pass. The updraft from the sea blew so hard there that people could jump over the cliff and land safely below, buoyed by the force of the wind.

I phoned Morena, the preacher, and my best man, shipmate Marvin Lokkesmoe. We had the ceremony on the Pali by the side of the road, as curious tourists stared and a gale-force wind glued my uniform and Morena's dress to our bodies. Later that evening, we were married again by Harold DeGroff.

Morena had known her bridesmaid, Rosa, only a few days. The altar was covered with orchids for which we paid ten dollars. The bill for the fifty-five-guest banquet was fifty-five dollars. I was twenty-seven and Morena was twenty-five.

We moved into an apartment for $32.50 a month. I was at sea at least half the time for the next six months, but when I was home, it was a great time for us newlyweds. We both participated in the Navigator ministry on weekends and thoroughly enjoyed serving together.

The world did its best to intrude on our happiness, however. Nazi Germany was bombing Britain and had invaded Russia. In July, Japan occupied French Indochina (South Vietnam). In response, President Roosevelt froze Japanese assets in America and ended oil sales to Japan. Civilian households in Honolulu were asked to store up a month's supply of food and water. Tensions were definitely rising.

As the end of 1941 approached, we recognized that the threat from Japan had increased, but we believed its most likely next targets were elsewhere in the Pacific, such as oil-rich Indonesia or Malaysia. We did not think the Japanese would be foolish enough to attack the United States. Certainly not for a while yet.

We were wrong.

★6★

FURY ON OAHU

THE COMMANDER'S TORPEDO BOMBER flew at nearly ten thousand feet. From his middle seat in the three-person air-craft, he examined the vast expanse of thick clouds below him. Moments later, an immense crimson ball emerged from behind the clouds, splitting the eastern sky with its rays. "Glorious dawn!" the commander said—in English, the language of his enemy. The sunrise was familiar and spectacular—it appeared exactly like his country's naval flag.

It was just past 6:30 a.m., December 7, 1941.

I would meet the commander, thirty-nine-year-old Mitsuo Fuchida, years later under much better circumstances, although the memory of this day was still fresh when we met. He was a smart and dedicated officer, two of the reasons he'd been chosen to lead Japan's surprise attack force against our fleet stationed at Pearl Harbor.

Fuchida had much on his mind that morning. No doubt the events onboard the aircraft carrier *Akagi* only an hour earlier still occupied his thoughts. The farewell salute to his commander, Vice Admiral Chuichi Nagumo, and Nagumo's final words: "I am counting on you." The last tap on the shoulder by attack planner and friend Lieutenant Minoru Genda, offering a wordless grin that said much. The decision to launch the attack force despite rough seas. The last-moment gift of a white headband from the senior petty officer on behalf of the squadron maintenance group: "They would like to accompany you to Pearl Harbor themselves. Please put it on and go with our wishes."

The *hachimaki* was still wrapped tightly around Fuchida's aviation cap when he tuned a radio direction finder. He worried that the cloud cover, though beneficial for hiding his planes, might be so thick that they would overfly Pearl Harbor. Flying in four formation groups behind Fuchida's bomber were forty-nine level bombers, forty torpedo bombers, fifty-one dive bombers, and forty-three Zero fighters. The first wave of the Japanese strike force was a little more than two hundred miles north of the Hawaiian island of Oahu. The pilots were closing the distance rapidly.

Jazz music filled Fuchida's ears. He instructed his pilot to home in on the beam from KGMB, a Honolulu station. Fuchida adjusted the dial, trying to fine-tune it further, and the music was replaced by a radio announcer's voice: "The weather on Oahu island is partially clear, with clouds covering the mountains."

Fuchida pulled out a memo pad and pencil and began scribbling. "The clouds' altitude is 3,500 feet," the announcer continued, "but with good visibility and a north wind at ten knots."

"We've got it!" Fuchida shouted. The weather was cooperating beautifully—clouds to obscure their approach and clearing skies over Oahu for the attack. Fuchida could not have asked for more. Success for the Japanese attack force was at hand.

Those of us stationed at Pearl Harbor certainly had our chances to uncover the unexpected arrival of warplanes that morning. One of them occurred at 7:02 a.m. at an army radar station near Kahuku Point on Oahu's northern tip. Radar was a new technology then. The system on Oahu had gone into operation only a couple of weeks earlier and still had frequent glitches. Army sergeants Joe Lockard and George Elliott were just finishing their shift when a blip flashed on their screen. It was larger than any they'd seen before.

Elliott called the army's information center. The only people on duty were the switchboard operator, Private Joe McDonald, and pursuit officer Lieutenant Kermit Tyler. Everyone else was at breakfast. Tyler eventually spoke with Lockard, but was unimpressed with Lockard's report. He knew that US aircraft carriers were at sea, so the blip might be navy planes. He also recalled hearing the radio on his way to work and remembered it stayed on all night whenever B-17s flew in from the coast, so the blip might be a squadron of Flying Fortresses. Either way, it didn't occur to Tyler that the unidentified planes might be unfriendly. He told Lockard, "Don't worry about it."

We missed another chance to understand what was happening in the harbor itself. Earlier that morning, ten miles from the mouth of Pearl Harbor, a group of Japanese submarines deployed five two-man midget submarines. Each midget sub was armed with two torpedoes. At 3:42 a.m., lookouts aboard the minesweeper *Condor* saw what looked like a periscope southwest of the Pearl Harbor entrance buoy and alerted the destroyer *Ward*. The *Ward* searched for two hours without success. Neither the *Condor* nor the *Ward* reported the sighting.

At 6:30 a.m., a supply ship contacted the *Ward* about a strange black object in the water. The *Ward's* helmsman spotted the object from about a mile away. It was headed toward the entrance to the harbor. Ten minutes later, *Ward* Skipper William Outerbridge sounded general quarters, gave pursuit, and from a distance of one hundred yards fired a ship's gun at the submarine—the first shot by either side in the war. It missed. The second shot struck the sub at the junction of the hull and conning tower. The damaged sub drifted into a pattern of the *Ward's* depth charges, apparently sinking the vessel and killing its crew.

In a brief message, Outerbridge reported these events to a navy watch officer: "We have dropped depth charges upon sub operating in defensive sea area." A series of phone calls and attempted phone calls among navy officials followed, eventually reaching Admiral Kimmel, who was commanding the Pacific Fleet. But since there had been many recent false submarine sightings in the area, Kimmel had doubts about the report. He decided to wait for verification before taking further action.

Yet another opportunity was missed in part because of the weather. On December 6, American code breakers intercepted and began deciphering a lengthy message to Japanese peace negotiators in Washington, D.C. A second message, intercepted on the morning of December 7, implied that a Japanese attack was imminent and that something would happen at 1 p.m. Washington time—7:30 a.m. in Hawaii. General George Marshall, the army chief of staff, scribbled a message to be sent in code to American outposts across the Pacific:

> Japanese are presenting at one pm eastern standard time today what amounts to an ultimatum also they are under orders to destroy their code machine immediately. Just what significance the hour set may have we do not know but be on alert accordingly. Inform naval authorities of this communication. Marshall.

At noon Washington time, the message was sent by radio to the Caribbean Defense Command, the Philippines, and the Presidio army base in San Francisco. But atmospheric conditions blocked radio messages to Honolulu. Colonel Edward French, the officer in charge of the War Department's Signal Center, decided to send the message to Hawaii via commercial telegram. It was not marked priority and did not arrive until 7:33 a.m. Honolulu time. A messenger boy picked it up along with a batch of other cables, got on his motorcycle, and started his deliveries. One of his first stops was a message for a doctor on Vineyard Street. He would get to the army delivery later.

★ ★ ★

At about the same time that the messenger got on his motor-cycle, Commander Fuchida peered with high-powered binocu-lars through a narrow opening in the clouds below. Suddenly he uttered a single word: "Ha!" Below him lay the tan beaches, green forests, and gray mountains of northern Oahu. Fuchida fired a single flare, indicating to the other squadrons that sur-prise had been achieved. The torpedo planes were to attack first.

His fighters did not immediately respond to the signal, so Fuchida fired a second flare. The commander of the dive bombers mistook the flares as a two-flare signal, indicating that surprise had been lost. That meant the dive bombers should initiate the attack.

Fuchida was angry when he saw both the torpedo planes and the dive bombers descend simultaneously, a mix-up despite weeks of careful planning. But, he realized, it didn't much mat-ter. Below him, in plain sight, just as the Japanese had antici-pated, our battleships were lying in a row. No American planes rose up to meet the attacking force. The Japanese could not miss.

It was time. At 7:49 a.m., Fuchida ordered his radio man to send the attack signal, the first syllable of *totsugekiseyo* ("charge"). "To! To! To!" The bombers and torpedo planes began their runs as the commander's plane swung toward the southwest edge of Oahu in order to circle around again. At 7:53, Fuchida had his man send another coded message: "Tora! Tora! Tora!" (Tiger! Tiger! Tiger!) The entire Japanese fleet learned that com-plete surprise had been achieved. No doubt about it—they had caught us sleeping.

Two minutes later, the first bombs fell at Hickam and Wheeler airfields and at Pearl Harbor itself. Fuchida's plane was among those that dropped bombs on the *Maryland*. The sky turned black from smoke as the commander continued to monitor the deadly work of his attack force, observing the damage to US battleships, destroyers, cruisers, planes, facilities, and men. He could not have missed the fatal eruption of the *Arizona*, the blows that turned the *Oklahoma* upside down, or the torpedoes that slammed into my home for the previous eight years, the *West Virginia*.

I imagine that he must have grinned with satisfaction.

My view of the carnage on Battleship Row—and my opinion of it—could not have been more different. It was about 8:30 a.m. when I picked myself up off the ground after the machine-gun attack from the low-flying Japanese plane. From my position near the officer's club and Merry Point, I was dismayed by what I saw. Our proud battleship fleet was in shambles.

All I could think was that I had to get to my ship. Since the motor launches weren't running, my friend Ken Watters and I, along with seven or eight other fellows, hurried on foot toward a ferry landing near the navy hospital. Once aboard the ferry for the short crossing to Ford Island and Battleship Row, I had a better view of the *West Virginia*. As many as nine torpedoes and a pair of unexploded, two-thousand-pound bombs that crashed onto the deck had done their work. In addition to smoke and fire, the most glaring damage was a 140-foot hole above the second deck on the port side.

The crew had counter-flooded on the starboard side to keep the ship from capsizing. She now rested on the bottom of the shallow harbor, part of her starboard side jamming the adjacent *Tennessee* against a quay wall.

Once on Ford Island, Ken Watters and I parted ways, he to the *Maryland* and I in the direction of the *West Virginia*. At the quay, I boarded the *Tennessee* and ran to the opposite railing. The deck of the *West Virginia* was more than ten feet away and five feet below me, listing at a six-degree angle. However, the barrel of one of the *Tennessee*'s five-inch guns at midship was extended across the water and just over the railing of the *West Virginia*. I climbed onto the barrel and slid down until I reached the deck of my ship.

I was aboard a nearly abandoned vessel. Our captain, Mervyn Bennion, had been mortally wounded during the first wave of the attack. Most of the crew that survived had evacuated, though a few remained. The main thrust of the fire had already moved from the bow to my position midship. Flames had engulfed the topside "ready lockers"—the airtight, watertight metal lockers that housed fifty rounds of ammunition for every gun. I immediately decided that these were my priority. If they blew, the secondary explosions would cause further damage.

Our power was gone, but someone had pulled a fire hose from the *Tennessee* to the deck of the *West Virginia*. The man was gone—perhaps he had been killed. But the fire hose still produced water pressure, so I picked it up and shot a stream of water at an endangered ready locker. The flame went out, so I turned to another ready locker. A few moments later, the flames

Chief Gunner's Mate Jim Downing, "Navigator No. 6," with Bible

Jim, age 2

"Mama's pet"—Jim as a young boy

The Downing family's country store in Plevna, Missouri, circa 1920

Jim (center, back row) with members of the "Navigators Gospel Team" from the crew of the *West Virginia*

Jim with shipmates in Seattle. Jim's playful personality is on display as he pulls his friends' hair.

Jim as young sailor

Jim and Morena

Jim and Morena on their wedding day

Jim (center) with fellow Navigators. Dawson Trotman, founder of The Navigators, is in the front row at left.

Watercolor of the *West Virginia*, Jim's first ship. The "Wee Vee" was among the battleships attacked at Pearl Harbor by a Japanese air raid on Sunday, December 7, 1941.

A Navigators gathering in Honolulu, 1951. Jim is center-right, second from the front.

U.S.S. PATAPSCO AOG-1

The crew of the USS *Patapsco*.
Jim captained this ship starting in 1952.

Lieutenant Jim Downing, the junior commanding officer in the Pacific Fleet

Jim inspecting the crew of the *Patapsco* with Admiral Bernard Biggs (right)

The faculty of the Merchant Marines Academy. Jim (front row, third from right) was assistant professor of naval science.

Jim Downing, age 100, at a birthday celebration at The Navigators headquarters, holding a birthday card drawn by cartoonist Chuck Asay returned to the first locker. I had to continually change targets to cool the most vulnerable spots.

One hundred feet from our stern, fire from the burning *Arizona* leaped skyward and spread via the oil in the water. Off our bow, the bottom of the upside down *Oklahoma* seemed strikingly out of place, her huge propellers stretching hopelessly into the air.

As I manned the fire hose, I noticed a crewman lying on the deck, eyes closed. Was he dead or just knocked out? I moved closer and recognized him. Like me, he was a gunner's mate, in turret three instead of turret two. It was difficult to stand on the slanted and oil-slicked deck, but I kept my balance and knelt beside him. With the hose in one hand, I curled my other hand behind the man's back and gently lifted. I was horrified to see only a bloody mass behind him. The back of his head was gone.

I slowly moved toward the stern to water down more areas. Several more bodies lay on the deck around me. No one else would be able to tell the parents of these men what had happened to their sons. I decided it was my responsibility to learn their names so I could report what I knew to their mothers and fathers. While still spraying with the hose, I went to each man, sometimes crawling, and read his nametag. The navy had equipped us with fireproof cords and tags, so I could still read the tags even when bodies had been badly burned. I tried to memorize them all.

A new threat emerged. The first wave of the Japanese attack was over; the second wave was about to begin. But fighter planes still filled the skies, shooting at anything that moved. The USS *Neosho*, a fuel tanker, was docked ahead of the sinking

California, not far from the *Oklahoma* and *Maryland*. Though the *Neosho* had unloaded most of its six million gallons of aviation fuel since arriving the day before, it still carried enough gasoline and vapor that a Japanese bullet in the wrong spot would create an explosion dwarfing anything seen so far. Trying to prevent this catastrophe, the crew of the *Neosho* had her underway, barely moving but headed across the narrow harbor to a safer berth at Merry Point.

I watched, fascinated and fearful, as the Japanese planes swarmed like bees toward the *Neosho*. I was only about four hundred yards away.

One of those bullets is going to hit pretty soon, I thought. *God, I'll be with you in a minute.*

The minute passed. My fire hose kept spraying. The *Neosho* kept inching farther into the harbor. The Japanese planes kept diving and firing. *God*, I thought, *I'll be with you in another minute.*

Another minute passed.

Suddenly my fear melted away, replaced by the most overwhelming sense of peace I'd ever felt. For the next half hour, until the *Neosho* docked at Merry Point, I expected to die in the next minute. I was sure I would be ushered into God's presence—and that was fine with me. Peace.

I once read that 92 percent of the things we worry about never happen. And yet it's often worry that drives our prayers. And when those prayers over our worries are met with silence?

We wonder whether God cares about us. We wonder whether God is truly there.

Does God respond to false alarms? I believe he doesn't. God is a realist, I think, and while he is always present to us and always active and in control, he is not bound to engage our anxieties. If we're not feeling the peace of God, I suspect we're not truly at risk.

Where there *is* real trouble, real danger, I believe God is present. He may not do what we want, but he will provide what we need in times of trouble.

We need *him*. We need *his peace*.

I needed that peace when the second wave of the Japanese attack struck a little before nine. Seventy-eight dive bombers, fifty-four high-altitude bombers, and thirty-five fighters concentrated the majority of their firepower on aircraft, airfields, and hangars across the island. Nevertheless, those of us on Battleship Row and around the harbor continued to take fire. In Dry Dock No. 1, bombs exploded on the battleship *Pennsylvania*. Other bombers hit the destroyers *Cassin* and *Downes* in the same dry dock. Onboard ammunition exploded. The *Cassin* rolled off her blocks and into the *Downes*.

The *Nevada* was the only battleship to get under way that morning. She was headed for the harbor exit when the Japanese second wave descended, showering her with bombs and bullets. A tremendous explosion erupted from inside the *Nevada*, sending flames and debris above the masts. To avoid blocking the channel opening, the *Nevada's* temporary captain ran her aground near the navy hospital.

The harbor was full of burning fuel oil that leaked from

damaged ships. The *Tennessee* wasn't going anywhere, but her crew turned on her propellers to drive the burning oil away. On a day full of terrible sights, the saddest for me was watching explosions blow sailors off their ships and into the water. When they came up for air, their bodies caught on fire—they were human torches.

Eventually, more men came aboard the *West Virginia* to remove the dead. I had never handled a body before and was challenged by the effort of trying to lift dead weight equaling my own. Arms and legs flopped sideways as I helped carry the bodies to a boat bound for the hospital morgue.

At last, the second wave of the Japanese attack ended. Our antiaircraft guns had shot down twenty-nine of the attacking planes. My feelings fluctuated. I grieved over the human massacre, the demolished ships, and the oil- and blood-soaked teakwood decks of the *West Virginia*. The longer I looked at the blackened and warped superstructure of my home, the more my feelings changed from grief to anger. I was angry at the unchecked ambition of a people who believed that their emperor was the descendant of a sun goddess and that his desire to rule the world was a divine mission. I was angry that the American government and military leaders we'd trusted had failed to warn us what would happen. I was angry that we had virtually ignored Japan's previous aggressions against us and other nations. As the philosopher George Santayana once said, "Those who cannot remember the past are condemned to repeat it."

My next response was resolve. If I ever achieved a position of authority, I decided then, we would never again be caught napping. I would never forget what happened here.

I also felt a strong sense of pride. All around me were men who had recognized what was happening, ignored the risk, and did what needed to be done. In most cases there were no officers to tell them what to do. They acted on instinct and did the right thing.

On the other hand, I was also deeply disappointed for myself and my new wife. I'd been married only a few months and had been separated from Morena for more than half that time. Now, clearly, we were at war. Who knew what would happen or how much time we'd still have together?

As these conflicting and distressing emotions battled for supremacy in my heart and mind, another returned to supersede the rest: peace. There was nothing I could do about the situation. God was in control; I realized I was content to let him handle it. I gave up worrying about what was happening and resumed my focus on what I could do right then.

The *West Virginia* was eventually engulfed in flames, though the few of us fighting the fires did succeed in preventing the ready lockers from exploding. When, finally, the flames died out, our ship was reduced to a pile of scrap iron.

It occurred to me that I was hungry. A while earlier, I'd handed my watch to a friend on the *Tennessee*, Gus Gustafson, so it wouldn't be bathed in fuel oil. Now I asked Gus if he knew anyone in the galley who would give me a sandwich. Gus took me to the galley on the *Tennessee*, where someone handed me what I was looking for. I glanced at the clock: 11:45 a.m. I couldn't believe it. I'd been so focused that the events of the last three hours felt like thirty minutes.

Time is a strange dimension. Thousands of individual hopes,

plans, and lives that had been years or decades in the making had been violently changed or tragically ended in one morning. When more time passed, what changes would I, my wife, my shipmates, and my country see? One thing was certain: Our futures had just taken a new course.

About this same time, less than two hundred miles to the north, Commander Fuchida's pilot guided their plane onto the deck of the Japanese aircraft carrier *Akagi*. Fuchida's was the final plane to return to the carriers. He'd spent the rest of the morning coordinating and observing the attacks, then picked up two last fighters that had been separated from their squadrons before all three planes winged away from Oahu.

Fuchida was already thinking ahead to another assault that afternoon. He made a mental list of priority targets: fuel-tank farms, repair and maintenance facilities, perhaps a ship or two that had been missed during the morning.

One of the first people to greet Fuchida on deck was his friend Lieutenant Genda, the attack planner. Genda smiled with elation as he shook Fuchida's hand. Soon, Fuchida was summoned to the bridge to give his report. "Four battleships sunk," Fuchida said. "I know this from my personal observation. Four [other] battleships damaged." He listed by berth and type the other ships damaged.

Admiral Nagumo spoke next: "Do you think that the US fleet could not come out from Pearl Harbor within six months?"

The question made Fuchida uneasy. Much depended on his answer. But he had to give his honest opinion: "The main force of the US Pacific Fleet will not be able to come out within six months." Nagumo nodded and grinned.

Another officer interjected: "Is the enemy in a position to counterattack the task force?"

Fuchida believed a new attack was vital, but he again answered honestly. "I believe we have destroyed many enemy planes," Fuchida said, "but I do not know whether we have destroyed them all. The enemy most probably could still attack the fleet."

The officer was silent. Fuchida was dismissed. A few minutes later, he sat down to eat a rice dumpling with bean paste, a typical Japanese meal before battle. The *Akagi* received a signal from another carrier: "*Soryu* and *Hiryu* are ready for takeoff." Preparations for the launch of another wave of planes from the *Akagi* herself were nearly complete.

Fuchida was ready. All that remained was the order to strike.

Then a series of flags went up the *Akagi's* mast—a new course signal. The Japanese fleet would turn for home, following the same course they'd used to arrive.

What stupidity, Fuchida thought. Japan had momentum. The enemy was in disarray. This was the time to exploit their advantage, not run away.

Fuchida rushed to the bridge. After saluting, he said to Nagumo, "Why are we not attacking again?"

Before Nagumo could speak, Rear Admiral Ryunosuke Kusaka answered: "The objective of the Pearl Harbor operation has been achieved. Now we must prepare for other operations ahead."

Fuchida was frustrated because he was a tactician. He wanted to maximize damage in the operation he was responsible for. But tactical moves aren't necessarily strategic moves. You can blow up an oil dump, but why would you? An oil dump will never attack you.

While Fuchida was focused on Pearl Harbor, his superiors were considering a bigger picture. Those "other operations" Kusaka had in mind were in service to a primary objective for Japan in 1941: to add the Philippines to its empire and to strengthen its position in the Western Pacific. Japan had (probably outdated) intelligence that led it to believe that we intended to defend the Philippines with our battleships, sinking Japanese transport ships whenever they made their move against the Philippines. Japan attacked Pearl Harbor to neutralize the battleships, considered the main force in a war fought at sea. Since our battleships had been put out of operation, the Japanese commanders concluded that their mission at Pearl Harbor was accomplished. Besides, they had only a four-hour window to meet their refueling tankers. It was time to move on.

Pearl Harbor was only one piece of a much grander plan for Japan to dominate the region. It would be accompanied by eight more Japanese attacks throughout the Pacific that day.

At 10:00 a.m. Honolulu time, Japan destroyed three ships— two British and one American—at port in Shanghai.

Also at 10:00, Japan began its invasion of Malaya, which ultimately surrendered the following February.

At 11:30, Japan commenced air attacks on strategic sites in Singapore, which surrendered the following February.

At 1:00 p.m., Guam was attacked, falling to the Japanese by December 10.

Also at 1:00, Japan attacked Wake Island, the site of an American base. The island was surrendered to the Japanese on December 23.

At 2:00, Japan attacked British Hong Kong. After about two weeks of fighting, it was surrendered to the Japanese on Christmas Day.

At 3:00, Japan launched an attack on the Philippines. Over five hundred aircraft pummeled every US airbase on the islands. American and Filipino forces held out until surrendering in May 1942.

At 11 p.m., Japan issued an ultimatum to Thailand, after a short battle, to allow Japan right of occupation and free passage of 100,000 Japanese soldiers through Thai territory to Burma.

Japan had a good day. With this series of attacks, they added much of Asia to their empire—specifically what they called the "southern resources area." To make a world empire they required rubber, tin, and oil (the United States, Britain, and the Netherlands had cut off their oil exports, so that Japan only had a fifteen-month supply). The overarching plan was to control territory closer to home, then conquer Midway Atoll, the Hawaiian Islands, and eventually invade the West Coast of the United States. They were careful not to destroy oil, dry docks, the industrial naval shipyard, and other resources at Pearl Harbor that they would need after their occupation.

In their eagerness to disable our fleet of battleships, Japan's military leaders underestimated the value of aircraft carriers. The war to come would soon show the significance of aviation as a weapon. All this was in the future, however. On the bridge of the *Akagi*, Kusaka's firm tone had left no room for debate. From the point of view of Japan's commanders, the surprise attack on Pearl Harbor was unquestionably a success.

★7★

A DIFFERENT WORLD

I WAS STILL FIGHTING FIRES on the *West Virginia* that fateful Sunday when one of my shipmates ran up to me. "Deacon," he said, "I was blown over the side when the first torpedo hit. I tried to swim ashore with my clothes on. I ran out of breath and was afraid I wasn't going to make it. I knew my shortness of breath was due to smoking. I prayed to God, 'If you will just give me enough breath to make it to shore, I will never smoke another cigarette.'"

My glance shifted from his eyes to his hand. In it he held a lighted cigarette, of which he seemed totally unaware. Apparently not all battlefield decisions stand the test of time.

Perhaps my shipmate could be forgiven for his muddled mind. The attack had left many on the island of Oahu uncertain and disoriented. Though the Japanese planes ended their onslaught at about ten in the morning, many believed that more airstrikes, even a land invasion, were imminent. I certainly thought it was possible. After being fooled once, none of us could afford to think otherwise.

The army shut down commercial broadcasting on Hawaii's KGMB and KGU radio stations at 11:42 a.m. to prevent new waves of enemy planes from homing in on the signal. That decision left the civilian population out of the loop—including Morena, who spent the rest of the day and long into the night listening to the police communicating over the commercial airwaves and wondering if I was still alive.

The navy and army sent out ships and planes to scout for the Japanese task force and a possible invasion force, with no success. The army's head man in Hawaii, Lieutenant General Walter Short, directed the island's defenses from a command post in an ordnance storage tunnel inside Aliamanu Crater. Others prepared for invasion on their own. Enlisted men established machine-gun nests at Hickam Field and foxholes at Schofield Barracks. On the *Nevada*, still grounded near the hospital, Marines on deck carried rifles. Another Marine detail established gun emplacements on the beach nearby. The plan was to hold the ship for as long as possible when the Japanese returned, then retreat into the Oahu hills.

At about 3 p.m., Admiral Kimmel received the warning telegram sent that morning from General Marshall. It had finally been delivered by the messenger boy, decoded, sent by uniformed messenger to General Short, and then relayed to the navy. Kimmel threw it in a wastebasket.

Despite the fear and chaos spread by the surprise attack, most people rallied and helped however they could. Boy Scouts fought fires, served coffee, and delivered messages. American Legion members turned out for patrol and sentry duty. Football players from Willamette University (who had squared off against the University of Hawaii the day before) and from San Jose State College (scheduled to play the following weekend) were issued weapons and assisted the police department in securing the island. A local doctor delivered plasma to island hospitals, then took more plasma from donors. When more than five hundred people showed up to donate, his team quickly ran out of containers. They sterilized Coca-Cola bottles to store the plasma.

Once I saw there was nothing more I could do on the *West Virginia*, I left the ship to visit the hastily established burn ward at the navy hospital. I'd heard that a friend, Claude Knuckles of the *California*, was there.

The "ward" was actually a section of the lawn outside the hospital. I was half a mile away when I noticed the odor of the wounded—it reminded me of a stockyard. More than a hundred men lay in the sunshine in rows of cots, their oil-soaked bodies mutilated by the morning's fires, many with arms and legs held in place by a suspension apparatus. I noticed little in the way of bandages; most had open wounds.

Despite their pain, few of the men moaned or groaned. I'm sure they were heavily sedated.

I found Claude and spoke with him briefly. He'd been aboard his ship, climbing up a ladder from the main deck, when a bomb hit and threw him into the air. When he came down, he thought he was still on the main deck, but the explosion had hurled him down a level to the second deck. Engulfed by heat and smoke, Claude rushed toward what he thought was the nearest exit and ran into a steel bulkhead. Fortunately, Claude would recover from his injuries.

Many of the men in cots were so badly burned that they were blind and didn't know what was going on. I decided to focus on these men. I got a notebook and pen and spoke to them individually, letting them know where they were and what had happened with the attack. I tried to give them hope, though I felt helpless myself. To each one who could talk, I said, "If you'll give me your parents' name and address and dictate a short note, I'll send it to them."

I was impressed by the similarity of responses for the letters—they were optimistic. "I'm going to be all right," said one. "Don't worry about me," said another. They knew they were in bad shape but didn't want to concern their families.

Most of the men I spoke to died that night.

From the hospital, I made my way to the naval receiving station. This was a facility for feeding and housing naval personnel who were transferring from one assignment to another. It had facilities for 350 men. In the hours after the attack, the number of homeless sailors from damaged or sunken ships swelled to two thousand. The galley crew worked heroically, operating from early morning to late at night in an attempt to feed us all. For the next several days, lines were so long that it was possible to get in only two meals a day.

The rest of the staff at the receiving station also worked promptly and efficiently. They collected and distributed all the clothes they could round up from military and civilian sources. I definitely needed a new wardrobe—I looked like I'd been bathing in crude oil. Our new attire was quickly covered with oil as well; it floated several inches deep throughout the harbor. (It took two years for crews to remove most of the oil. The *Arizona* still leaks oil today.) We were instructed to dump washable soiled clothing into designated barrels, while other barrels contained clean laundry. Each man foraged for his own apparel, the result rarely a good fit. In our unmatched, ill-fitting "uniforms," we were a ragtag navy.

The receiving station opened its store and gave out what supply it had of bathroom gear. I had to share a toothbrush with my friend Marvin Lokkesmoe, better known as "Lokki," for several days.

At the navy's clothing store, we helped ourselves to a mattress, pillow, and blanket. A sports arena had just been completed near the base for the fleet's athletic events. This became our temporary home—we made our beds on the bleacher seats. The arena was soon renamed the "Mosquito Bowl" by those of us who slept there. The insects seemed to arrive from all over the island to enjoy the opportunity to feast.

Late that afternoon, the Hawaii governor announced that the islands were under military rule. The military established a curfew and blackout. The effectiveness of the blackout was questionable, however, since the *Arizona* continued to burn and erupt like Hawaii's Mauna Kea volcano for three days and nights. The flames were visible for fifty miles.

Despite the discomfort of the bleachers and mosquitoes, it didn't take me long to fall asleep. I was exhausted and still in a state of shock. The worst part was the uncertainty. As I drifted off, I realized that we'd suffered a terrible blow, but the great majority of our nation's resources were still intact. The fight against Japan was coming. Only God knew what would happen next.

On Monday, December 8, America awoke to a different world. Censors began screening messages sent to other nations by cable or radio. Christmas leaves were canceled for military personnel. Borders closed and roadblocks arose. Government officials rounded up Japanese nationals, eventually detaining them in internment camps. Private aviation was canceled and licenses suspended. Armed guards were suddenly visible everywhere.

The debate between isolationists and those who favored an active response to the world's militaristic nations was over. America was going to war.

Rumors of impending attacks on the West Coast abounded. In Washington state, navy officials at a Puget Sound base announced they would shoot down any plane flying overhead. In San Francisco, fishing boats were ordered to stay at anchor, and the lights on the Golden Gate Bridge were turned off. On the Bay Bridge, cars with Japanese passengers were stopped and the occupants questioned. In Los Angeles, four thousand anti-aircraft troops were deployed, as guards watched over the new aqueduct. Cargo ships up and down the coast were "bottled up."

A few minutes after noon in Washington, D.C., President Franklin Delano Roosevelt departed the White House for the Capitol. A few minutes later, Speaker of the House Sam

Rayburn welcomed the president to the floor of the House of Representatives. As Roosevelt ascended a ramp to the dais, members of Congress, normally divided by politics, rose from their seats and gave him the most enthusiastic ovation they'd ever delivered. Some of them cried.

Roosevelt looked tired, but he spoke in a clear, measured, tone:

Yesterday, December 7, 1941—a date which will live in infamy—the United States was suddenly and deliberately attacked by naval and air forces of the Empire of Japan.

The United States was at peace with that nation and, at the solicitation of Japan, was still in conversation with its government and its Emperor looking toward the maintenance of peace in the Pacific. . . . It will be recorded that the distance of Hawaii from Japan makes it obvious that the attack was planned many days or even weeks ago. During the intervening time the Japanese government has deliberately sought to deceive the United States by false statements and expressions of hope for continued peace. . . .

As Commander-in-Chief of the Army and Navy I have directed that all measures be taken for our defense. Always will we remember the character of the onslaught against us. No matter how long it may take us to overcome this premeditated invasion, the American people in their righteous might will win through to absolute victory.

I believe I interpret the will of Congress and of
the people when I assert that we will not only defend
ourselves to the uttermost but will make very certain
that this form of treachery shall never endanger us
again.

Hostilities exist. There is no blinking at the fact that
our people, our territory, and our interests are in grave
danger. With confidence in our armed forces—with
the unbounding determination of our people—we will
gain the inevitable triumph—so help us God.

I ask that our Congress declare that since the
unprovoked and dastardly attack by Japan on Sunday,
December 7, 1941, a state of war has existed between
the United States and the Japanese Empire.

Back at Pearl Harbor, those of us who remained were adjust-
ing to a new normal. Since I'd been anticipating a return to the
mainland, I had recently withdrawn all of my and Morena's
money—$450—from our bank in Honolulu and put it in the
post office safe aboard the *West Virginia*. The safe did not survive the attack, and neither did my personal effects, notebooks,
other valuable papers, or our money. All we had left was a few
dollars in Morena's purse.

Fortunately, the disbursing officer's safe aboard ship was on
a deck above the flooding. It was fireproof as well. On Monday
morning, a crew returned to the ship and opened the safe with
a metal-burning torch. The disbursing officer, Ensign Vance
Fowler, retrieved several hundred thousand dollars and placed
it in a safe on shore. He set up a temporary office and began

taking sworn statements from sailors to make new pay records, which would allow him to give us an advance.

Fowler and I were good friends. I did business with him daily. One day he'd shown me a letter from his mother. She included a verse of Scripture in every letter. "Deacon," he said, "I bet you five dollars this is one Bible passage you don't know." The verse was 2 Chronicles 7:14.

I replied, "Does it go something like this? 'If my people, which are called by my name, shall humble themselves, and pray, and seek my face, and turn from their wicked ways—'"

Fowler stood, slammed the letter on his desk, and said, "I give up. You know every verse in the Bible." I enjoyed the look on his face a few moments before finally admitting that this was one of the best-known verses in the Old Testament and probably the only verse in 2 Chronicles I knew.

On that Monday, when it was my turn to approach Fowler's desk to request a salary advance, his face turned pale and he began to breathe heavily. He stood and ran his hands up and down my arms. "Deacon," he said, "am I ever glad to see you."

"I'm glad to see you too," I said, "but we've never had a ceremony like this before."

Fowler shook his head. "Do you know who walked out the door just before you came in? It was the chaplain. He told me he had just buried you."

We figured out that there was a gunner's mate in the fifth division with the same name as mine. He had been killed in the attack. The chaplain had presided over his burial.

Later that day, I was on the other end of a case of "back from the dead." On Sunday, bodies of the fallen had been laid in rows on Ford Island. Since everyone had ID tags, it was easy to make a list of the victims. Some of them, however, weren't dead; they had been knocked unconscious by the tremendous concussion from the explosions. When they regained consciousness later, they simply got up and walked away.

So on Monday, I found myself confused as I stood in a food line behind a man who looked like David Secor, our Marine barber. It couldn't be David. I'd heard directly from a man who'd hauled his body to Ford Island that David was dead. I looked this man in the eye—it *was* David. Now I knew how Jesus' disciples had felt when they met him two days after the crucifixion.

Even though the *West Virginia* was sidelined, I was still postmaster, and I still had duties to perform. On Monday morning, I set up my open-air USS *West Virginia* post office on the navy landing across from Merry Point. Lokki got some plywood from the submarine-base carpenter shop and built a sorting case for me. It was almost exactly the same spot where the Japanese pilot had tried to kill us the morning before.

Although telephones were restricted to urgent and emergency calls, Lokki phoned Morena for me. If she brought her military ID card, he said, she might be able to get on the base. She did and was allowed through. I was wearing an oil-soaked uniform, my hair was full of oil, and I hadn't shaved. Morena didn't mind. "I've never been more glad to see you," she said, "in spite of your look."

I needed a way to get back and forth between my new "office" and the base post office, but vehicles were in short supply. I asked the navy yard supply officer to issue me a bicycle. He refused, saying the *West Virginia* was sunk and he had no account to charge it to. There is a time to go by the book and a time to adjust to changing circumstances. I talked with one of our ship's officers, who apparently got through to the supply officer. I received a message that a bicycle was waiting for me.

The *West Virginia* lost 105 men in the attack. By name, at least, I knew them all. Many of these men had mail, some of it Christmas packages from home. For censorship purposes, I was not allowed to explain why their mail was being returned. I simply had to stamp the returning mail "Unknown." One of these was for Captain Bennion, a good man. Several days later, I received a letter from his wife. I'd returned his mail to her, marked "Unknown." She wrote to explain that he'd been killed in action, which of course I already knew.

Sorting, forwarding, and returning mail occupied most of my days during those first weeks of the new war. The navy had an efficient personnel records system, however. Within forty-eight hours of the attack on Pearl Harbor, most families had been notified if their husband or son was reported dead or missing.

The list of notifications was long. By at least one account, 2,403 Americans lost their lives on December 7: 2,008 navy personnel, 218 army personnel, 109 Marines, and 68 civilians. Nearly half of the deaths occurred instantly—over a thousand men—when the *Arizona* blew up at about 8:10 a.m. More than 1,100 people were wounded.

The damage to ships, planes, and facilities was shattering as well. Eighteen ships were sunk or seriously impaired. Mostly on the ground, 188 planes were destroyed and another 159 damaged. Installations and airfields at Hickam, Wheeler, Ford Island, Kaneohe, and Ewa also suffered extensive damage.

The losses were more than just statistics, of course. Each death was heartbreaking for the victim's family and friends. My own loss of friends, the rows of bodies, and the threat of new attacks certainly had an impact on me and my living comrades. Death surrounded us. The new war forced my shipmates to confront their mortality and their status with God, in some cases for the first time. Japan's surprise attack influenced them far more than my most stirring words.

For me, the war only increased the urgency I felt to lead others to faith in Christ. On the Tuesday after the attack, I started an evening Bible study in an unlit basement at the naval receiving station. The nightly gathering grew so quickly that we had to move to an air raid shelter on Ford Island. We continued meeting each evening for the next three months, attracting as many as forty people per night. Later, I received letters from more than a hundred military men who'd attended these sessions, each telling me he'd become a Christian and how glad he was to have made that choice.

I was encouraged by what was happening. In the midst of a terrible time, God was fulfilling a promise from Scripture: "And we know that all things work together for good to them that love God, to them who are the called according to his purpose."

Perhaps no empire had expanded so much and so quickly by force of arms as Japan. We and our allies, the British, had underestimated our new enemy and now faced a long and difficult fight. To make matters worse, Germany declared war against the United States on December 11.

My world had changed. The future appeared grim. And yet I was not worried. It wasn't that I was naive. I knew that I might die in the battle ahead. And it wasn't my confidence in America's military and our country's resolve to see the fight through, though I strongly believed in both.

No, it was something else. A few days before the attack, I'd read an account by a soldier of his experience a few months earlier as a member of the British Expeditionary Force (BEF). In May 1940, thousands of British, French, and Belgian troops in France were nearly surrounded by German forces. The allies withdrew to the port city of Dunkirk, hoping to evacuate as many troops as possible across the channel to England. Over a period of eight days, almost 340,000 men were rescued by a hastily assembled fleet of over eight hundred boats, a combination of navy and merchant marine ships and civilian vessels pressed into duty: fishing boats, auto ferries, pleasure craft, and lifeboats. The operation is known as the Miracle of Dunkirk.

Though the Germans were initially slow to respond to the evacuation, they did not stand by and watch. On May 31, they bombed the city of Dunkirk. They also bombed and strafed Allied troops on the beaches and in the boats as they attempted to escape.

One of the BEF soldiers on the beach was a Christian. After one of the strafing runs, he said, "We can't dodge them. We might as well have some fun." He organized a soccer tournament, with six teams of troops competing against each other between the German attacks. The soldier was not worried about his dire circumstances. Instead, he said later, "I had the deepest peace that I'd ever had in my life."

I believe that soldier was describing what I was feeling when I prayed, "God, I'll be with you in a minute. God, I'll be with you in another minute." When I expected my life to end, I experienced the greatest peace I had *ever known*. The Lord was with me during my worst moments at Pearl Harbor. I understood then that he would *always* be there.

★ 8 ★

NO SACRIFICE TOO GREAT

JAPAN'S SURPRISE ATTACK on Pearl Harbor and the outbreak of war led to sacrifices across America both small and large. Patriotic posters urged citizens to "Do with less—so they'll have enough." The American people responded by purchasing war bonds and by conducting drives to collect scrap metal, aluminum cans, and rubber for the military. In spring 1942, the government instituted a nationwide rationing program so more resources could be devoted to the fight. Families used ration stamps to buy their allotment of meat, sugar, fat, butter, vegetables, fruit, clothing, gasoline, tires, fuel oil, and more.

The nation's sacrifices extended beyond materials. Thousands of men left their families to enlist in one of the services, including celebrities such as baseball star Bob Feller (navy) and movie idol Clark Gable (army air forces). Because of the sudden short-age of manpower, women began taking jobs in defense plants as welders, electricians, and riveters.

For Morena and me, and for many others already part of the US military establishment, the sacrifices demanded by the war were immediate and personal. I wasn't permitted to move back home or even visit. I was able to see Morena briefly on or near the base only a few times that December. I anticipated being sent out to sea soon on another ship.

Before our marriage, I'd been blunt about the life Morena was signing up for: "The fact is," I said, "in my life, it's Jesus first and the military second. You are third." When you're young and in love, you can go along with a statement like that. But a few months into our marriage, Morena reached her limit. She wanted to plan a Bible study for an evening I had to be aboard the *West Virginia*. When I explained there was nothing I could do, she said, "I *hate* the navy!" Military life can be hard on families.

Now, only five months after exchanging wedding vows, we were about to find out just how hard it could be. Civilian personnel not vital to the war effort were instructed to return to the mainland. Given my uncertain future, we reluctantly agreed that it was for the best. Morena was notified to report to the luxury liner *Lurline*, which was being converted to a troop ship. It was scheduled to depart for Los Angeles on Christmas Day, 1941.

December 25 was even warmer than usual for winter in Honolulu—the temperature would reach 85 degrees. The war news did not match our sunny skies, however. Marines had val-iantly held off Japanese invaders for two weeks at Wake Island, but now communication had been cut off and the island had to be considered lost. Hong Kong had just fallen. American troops at Manila in the Philippines were virtually surrounded, prompting a statement from the US War Department: "Though American and Philippine troops are greatly outnumbered, they are offering stiff resistance to the Japanese forces in a series of delaying actions." Delaying actions meant the inevitable was near.

I didn't feel much like celebrating Christmas, not that I had the opportunity. We were on double alert since we thought the Japanese might choose this day to launch another attack. Morena had to report to the *Lurline* at noon, so she borrowed a friend's car and drove to Pearl Harbor late in the morning to see me one last time. She wasn't allowed on the base that day. I met her in a parking lot near a row of bungalows that housed navy personnel.

Her suitcases were packed and ready in the car. Morena was wearing a formal dress for travel. We stood face to face, her lips pressed tight together. There was nothing else to do but say good-bye.

"This is the saddest day of our marriage," she said.

"I know it," I said. "Who knows what's going to happen? We'll just have to see what works out."

"I'll pray for you every day," she said, tears forming in her eyes.

I felt my own eyes watering and found it difficult to speak. "I'll do the same," I said.

After an all-too-brief hug and kiss, she was gone.

For the second time that month, we'd parted wondering if we'd ever see each other again. I would not lay eyes on my wife for another year and a half, more than triple the length of time we'd been married. That good-bye in the parking lot was one of the toughest moments of our lives to date, but our situation was hardly unique. We were realists. Everyone had to sacrifice.

Morena arrived safely in Los Angeles. She stayed for a few days to visit friends and fellow Navigators, then drove our 1937 Chevrolet to Little Rock, Arkansas, to be with her parents. Since the gasoline ration was three gallons a week, she had to get special gas coupons for the trip.

People were worried about the new war, but also angry and ready to play their part. In Little Rock, public rallies were held to sell war bonds. The promoters needed a celebrity. Morena became that celebrity. No one else in Little Rock had been on the scene when the Japanese attacked.

Morena had previously demonstrated her desire to aid the war effort by giving blood at Pearl Harbor. We already associated the island with blood, actually: The Hawaiian name of the conference center where we had been married, Kokokahi, means "of one blood." Now the significance was more profound. After the attack Morena lined up alongside Filipinos, Chinese, Japanese, native Hawaiians, and other Americans to donate. The technicians did not record races or nationalities as they drew blood. They labeled only the blood type. The rest didn't matter. This view was in keeping with the apostle Paul, who told the Athenians at Mars Hill that God had made "of one blood" all the nations that dwell on earth. But it was quite a contrast to the racial attitudes of Germany's führer, Adolf Hitler, who revealed his views about America not long after Christmas Day: "Everything about the behavior of American society reveals that it's half Judanized, and the other half Negrified. How can anyone expect a State like that to hold together?"

Naval intelligence had instructed Morena to limit her comments about the Pearl Harbor attack to what had already been released to the press. But that didn't seem to concern the promoters in Little Rock. They invited her to speak at luncheons and banquets, urging people to support the war effort. Newspapers showed her picture with captions such as "She Was There. Her Husband Fought at Pearl Harbor. She Gave Blood to the Wounded."

Morena wasn't satisfied with just these activities, however. She soon got permission from the superintendent of the Women's State Prison of Arkansas to hold Bible studies with the inmates. It was a fruitful ministry that gave her compassion for women prisoners. Years later, Morena would start a ministry for inmates at the Colorado State Prison for Women.

Back at Pearl Harbor, the navy kept my fellow sailors and me busy, which was in many ways a blessing. We lived day to day and tried not to think about the future.

It turned out that instead of being transferred to another ship, I joined my crewmates in working to restore the *West Virginia* for action. Early in 1942, I was promoted to the rank of chief gunner's mate.

To get around more quickly at the base, I gave up my bicycle and bought an old car from a shipmate for a hundred dollars. Since tires were sold only by special permit, I drove on three bald, regular-sized tires and one much-larger balloon tire.

We were of course keenly interested in any reports on developments in the war, particularly in the Pacific. During those first months of 1942, the news was nearly all bad. In February, Japan took Singapore and won the Battle of the Java Sea, leading to its occupation of the Dutch East Indies. On April 9, US troops on Bataan surrendered to the Japanese. We finally received a good report when we learned of a daring raid led by Army Air Corps Lieutenant Colonel Jimmy Doolittle. On April 18, fifteen of sixteen B-25 Mitchell bombers dropped their payloads on targets in and near Tokyo, showing that Japan was vulnerable. Morale was boosted among the allies around the world.

May brought the Battle of the Coral Sea, which included two days of intense airstrikes between Japanese and Allied navies. We lost the aircraft carrier *Lexington*, as well as other ships, planes, and men. But Japan also suffered serious losses, and its intention to invade Port Moresby in New Guinea was thwarted.

Though I remained at Pearl, the Battle of the Coral Sea involved many friends, including a former baker from New Jersey. In 1938 at a YMCA in Bremerton, I'd spoken to a group of sailors about Jesus and asked if any wanted to give their lives to Christ. Vic McAnney came forward. Vic and I hit it off. He was a handsome, winsome guy whom everyone liked. Since Vic was three or four years younger than I and newer to his faith, I helped him grow spiritually. We attended many Christian conferences together. Our relationship reminded me of the Bible's David and Jonathan—we were like brothers. I'd never had a better friend.

In 1942, Vic served as a baker on the *Astoria*, a heavy cruiser assigned to the carrier *Yorktown*, and had become the spiritual leader on that ship. He wrote in a letter to his fiancée,

I am learning more and more to live moment by moment yielded to [God]. I am learning, or should I say realizing, more and more that I am in the greatest field of service there is for me now. I am glorying in the fact that I know the Lord and have the privilege of serving Him here among such hungry hearts.

The *Astoria, Yorktown,* and other ships that fought in the Coral Sea returned to Pearl Harbor after the battle. The *Yorktown* was badly damaged. I met with the Navigator ministry leader aboard the carrier. "I'm sure glad to be back," he said. "We all could use a period of less stress and more fellowship. It will take a month for them to make repairs." The task force commander, Admiral Chester Nimitz, had other plans, however. Over the weekend, crews patched up the flight deck with wood timbers. Within seventy-two hours of their arrival, the *Yorktown, Astoria,* and other members of the task force were back at sea. They were headed to a destination thirteen hundred miles northwest: Midway Island.

The Japanese intended to lure our Pacific fleet into a trap at Midway. What they didn't know, however, was that American code breakers had deciphered multiple messages and learned of the plan. We laid a trap of our own. Though Japan had superior ship numbers, including four aircraft carriers, the United States recorded one of the most decisive naval victories in history. All four Japanese aircraft carriers were sunk, and Japanese losses in manpower were ten times those of the United States.

The one major loss for us was the *Yorktown.* I believe our Navigator leader survived that battle. Many others did not.

We didn't know it at the time, but the Battle of Midway was the turning point of the war in the Pacific. Japan never fully recovered from its loss of ships, planes, and experienced personnel. Nevertheless, the fight to subdue Japan over the next three years would be brutal and costly—for the nation and for me personally. I was frequently reminded that each of us might be called to make the ultimate sacrifice at any time.

I stumbled across one of those reminders shortly after the Midway conflict. Back at Pearl Harbor, work crews were slowly pumping water out of the bowels of the *West Virginia*, a process that would take many days. I wanted to see if anything was left of my post office, in particular the safe that contained my personal funds and about $10,000 in government money. I grabbed a flashlight, went on board, and ventured alone belowdecks.

The passageways were pitch-black and eerie. The sound of water lapping faintly below echoed off the bulkheads around me. It was like descending into a swamp—or maybe a tomb.

As I stepped down what we sailors called a ladder (really a metal stairway), the sounds of water got louder. I knew I was nearing the water level and would soon be forced to stop. I lowered my foot to what I thought was the next step. My shoe suddenly slid two or three feet and I nearly fell. Quickly, I aimed my flashlight where I'd stepped, just in time to see a man's body before it disappeared into a black mixture of seawater and oil. My shoe had slid along the man's decomposing leg, exposing skin to the bone.

Unnerved, I hurried up and off the ship. I didn't mention the incident to anyone. I knew that others had been assigned to scour the ship for bodies and they'd eventually locate this one.

Of the 105 attack victims from the *West Virginia*, seventy would be found belowdecks.

A couple of days later, I recovered my courage and again attempted to locate the post office. More water had been pumped out, so I was able to go deeper into the ship. I'd heard that another detail had discovered an unexploded, eighteen-hundred-pound Japanese bomb below decks, so I was extra careful. At one point I came around a corner and found a Marine seated in the passageway. "I hear there's an unexploded bomb on the ship," I said. "Do you know where it is?"

The Marine stood up, revealing his "chair"—it was the bomb. He'd drawn the unfortunate duty of guarding it. Once again I terminated my search for the post office.

Later, I tried once more. This time enough water had been removed for me to reach my goal. Unfortunately, there was nothing left of my former office. A torpedo had ripped through the ship's outer wall, opening a 140-foot hole and blowing out the bulkheads where my office was supposed to be. I could see all the way down the deck. If I'd been on duty and at my post that day, I'd have been killed immediately.

There was no sign of the safe. On another visit, I examined the spot where the torpedo had penetrated the outer wall and curled the metal underneath the entry point so that it bent down to the deck. Wrapped in the curved metal was a pad of postage stamps. It was the only trace of my former duties and possessions.

A day or two after finding my old office, I heard disturbing news. A crew on the *West Virginia* had opened up a compartment far below decks that was surrounded by water. They discovered a dry storeroom. Inside were dead flashlight batteries, empty emergency ration containers, a calendar, and three bodies. I didn't know them personally, but I recognized the names of two of them from my duties as postmaster: Ronald Endicott, an eighteen-year-old from Aberdeen, Washington, and Louis "Buddy" Costin, twenty-one, from Indiana. Apparently the men had been trapped there during the attack, the pressure of the water too great for them to open the doors and try to escape. The calendar was open to the month of December. A handwritten red "X" filled each day from December 7 through December 23. That was the day the men must have run out of oxygen. They'd nearly made it to Christmas.

I tried to imagine what it had been like for these two in that small room, running out of heat, food, and air, the days passing. I was sure they'd suffered. It was a tragedy.

In June and July 1942, I attempted to turn my thoughts away from death. I enjoyed meeting with my friend Vic and hearing about the wonderful work God was doing in men's hearts on the *Astoria*. Vic and his crewmates shipped out of Pearl on July 14 to take part in Operation Watchtower, the invasion of Guadalcanal and Tulagi in the lower Solomon Islands. Later I learned that Vic was an active participant in the nightly Bible classes aboard the *Astoria*, with as many as three men an evening committing their lives to Christ.

On August 6, Vic was up most of the night baking bread for the hundreds of sandwiches being prepared for the men during the upcoming operation. There was little time on this night for fellowship or Bible study. On August 7, the *Astoria* supported Marine landings on Guadalcanal and other islands. It was about

1:50 a.m. on August 9 when a bugle blew the general quarters call. A Japanese task force led by Vice Admiral Gunichi Mikawa had snuck by Savo Island and surprised our ships. Vic was at his battle station as an ammunition handler for antiaircraft guns. The first four Japanese salvos missed their target, but the fifth tore into the *Astoria's* superstructure. Within minutes, the ship was an inferno. The *Astoria* sank a little after noon.

When I heard about the fate of the *Astoria*, my heart sank as well. I began asking around. Soon my fears were confirmed: Vic was dead, likely killed in that first Japanese salvo. My friend and brother in Christ was gone. The chaplain on the *Astoria* told me that he'd seen Vic's body after he'd been killed and that he had "the sweetest smile on his face I'd ever seen on any human being."

I later learned about a statement Vic wrote to his fiancée:

I have begun to read the book *Caleb the Overcomer*, and so far it is really good. [It includes] the expression, "The best incentive to live such a life is to see someone living it." In that light, Jim Downing is my Caleb. He is the one who came to my mind when I read that part. His life means more to me than all the sermons I have ever heard!

I lost many other friends before and after that time. Another heavy blow struck in November. Jack Armstrong, a husky football and boxing enthusiast from Minnesota, was a friend, a Navigator serving as a spiritual mentor aboard the light cruiser *Atlanta*. When *Atlanta's* task force was attacked during the Battle of Guadalcanal, Jack was at his battle station near the bridge. One leg was blown off and the other filled with shrapnel. After the captain called for medics, Jack said they should treat the non-Christians first.

Jack didn't recover from his terrible injuries. That previous September he had by chance run into a mutual friend, LaVerne Tift, in the Tonga Islands. During their conversation, Jack said, "Tift, God has been talking to me and let me know that when I go out into battle this time, I am not coming back. I have written to my mother, brother, and many friends. I've even given instructions as to what should be done with my personal things. In all this I have no fear. Many are coming to Christ on the ship and they will carry on. God has given me this verse for an anchor: 'Fear thou not; for I am with thee: be not dismayed; for I am thy God: I will strengthen thee; yea, I will help thee; yea, I will uphold thee with the right hand of my righteousness.'"

I searched the cemeteries on Oahu for Vic and Jack, hoping that their bodies had been recovered and buried there. I wanted to say good-bye.

I didn't find either one.

As devastating as these losses were, I took comfort in the knowledge that my Christian friends were experiencing the joy of an eternal reunion with Jesus and each other. My mission remained to introduce as many others as possible to the God who had prepared a place for them in heaven.

As we built up a new crew for the *West Virginia*, we were able to assemble a new team for Bible study and outreach. I coordinated with Harold DeGroff, still the Navigator director in Honolulu, in leading sessions for the men. I taught

Sunday-morning classes for high schoolers at the Honolulu Bible Training School. In the midst of the grim reality of world war, our efforts gave us hope and the satisfaction of doing meaningful work. I couldn't imagine anything more rewarding.

Meanwhile, the tides of war were slowly shifting in our favor. Hitler had miscalculated when he invaded Russia in June 1941. After early victories, the German offensive stalled. In November 1942, Russia launched Operation Uranus, using its troops to encircle hundreds of thousands of German, Romanian, Italian, and Hungarian troops in and near Stalingrad. In February 1943, out of food and ammunition, the remaining Axis troops at Stalingrad surrendered. Hitler's two-front war cost Germany momentum, materials, and men.

The Guadalcanal campaign, our first major offensive in the Pacific, resulted in the evacuation of remaining Japanese troops from the area in February 1943. Though we suffered many losses, the impact on Japan's forces was even greater. We also now commanded an important strategic area.

The *West Virginia* was getting closer to joining the fight. In May 1943, the ship was sufficiently repaired so that we could complete sea trials. We soon set off for Bremerton under the escort of an old destroyer equipped with armaments and depth charges for fighting any Japanese submarine that might try to attack us.

When I learned we'd be returning to the mainland, I contacted Morena via a code we'd devised. In a letter, I suggested she visit our Navigator contact in Bremerton and listed the dates when I thought she should go. It got past the censors, and Morena was able to learn I was headed for Bremerton. She and a friend drove our Chevrolet from Little Rock to Los Angeles. Then another friend accompanied Morena up the West Coast. When the *West Virginia* tied up at the pier in Bremerton, there she stood, along with a few hundred other wives and children.

Sadly, our first reunion in a year and a half lasted only a few minutes. I still remember how the look of joy on Morena's face changed to disappointment when I explained I had to go immediately to the post office to pick up and process what turned out to be several hundred pounds of ship's mail. I felt terrible but there was nothing I could do; I had to put my postal duties first.

It took two days to handle and distribute all that mail. Finally, however, I was able to join Morena in the apartment she'd rented. It was so small that there wasn't room for the dining table and bed to be set up at the same time. We didn't mind. We were just happy to be together again.

Months of separation and a tiny living space seemed like small sacrifices to make when everyone around us was giving up the same or more, and still others were advancing the cause at the cost of their lives. Author Walter Lord wrote in *Day of Infamy*, his book about the Pearl Harbor attack, that "it was a day when rank was forgotten, when all that counted was a good idea, when people only wanted to pitch in together."

That was the spirit of the time—everyone wanted to pitch in and do his or her part to defeat our enemies. No sacrifice was considered too great. Our families, our futures, and our lives were at stake. This was a fight we simply had to win.

★9★

THE BUCK STOPS HERE

I'D BEEN IN BREMERTON less than a month when I received new orders. I was to report to the New Construction Gunner's Mate School at the Naval Gun Factory in Washington, D.C. After graduation I would be sent to a new ship.

I can't say I looked forward to an assignment with another crew, but I accepted it. I hurriedly wound up my affairs as postmaster and with a certain amount of sadness left the mighty ship that had been my home for the past ten years.

We were given twenty days and enough gas rations to make the cross-country car trip. Everything we owned fit in the two-door Chevrolet. To conserve fuel and rubber tires, travel was not allowed after sunset, and gasoline was not sold at night. The national speed limit was thirty-five miles per hour.

Only a few days before we left, I received another surprise—Morena was pregnant. This was a much more exciting development for both of us. Since I was nearly thirty and Morena was twenty-seven, we weren't exactly youngsters. We felt it was time to start a family.

Morena's new circumstances and appetite for two added a few complications to our trip. In Salt Lake City, we stopped at a restaurant for a breakfast of bacon, eggs, toast, and jelly while getting our car lubed and the oil changed. By the time we got to the other side of town, Morena was ready to eat again. I kidded her, saying, "We just ate two hours ago." "I know," she said. "But I'm hungry." This time we stopped at a sandwich shop. We were both learning about the needs of a pregnant mother.

While crossing Kansas, we ran low on gas as darkness approached. With no gas station in sight, we had to park on the side of the road and sleep in the car. It was particularly hard for Morena since we had no prospect for a meal until the next day.

Our trip included a stopover with the Downing family in Missouri. My former pastor knew I'd been promoted to chief gunner's mate, but he spread the word that I was chief officer of the navy. My new uniform may have convinced a few people he was telling the truth. Instead of my all-white sailor's shirt and pants, I now wore a combination cap, double-breasted blue coat with eight brass buttons, white shirt, and tie.

My parents were thrilled to see us and meet Morena for the first time. Donald, my older brother, was now a pilot with the Army Air Corps in the Pacific. A.J., my younger brother, was a B-17 Flying Fortress pilot. During the war, A.J. was shot down twice, but he eventually completed thirty-five missions over Germany. I was proud of them both, as were my parents, but it was especially worrisome for my mother to have her three children in harm's way. We were all sad when it was time to go. Saying good-bye reminded me of my departure for Hannibal and the navy eleven years before, except this time my mother was very brave—there were no tears.

Morena and I eventually completed our three-thousand-mile journey. Neither of us had been to Washington, D.C., so on the drive into the city we were thrilled when the Capitol Dome, Washington Monument, and Lincoln and Jefferson memorials came into view. We rented a small apartment near the gunner's mate school.

My class hours for the monthlong course of study were 8 a.m. to 4:30 p.m., Monday through Friday. We learned about the navy's new dual-purpose surface and antiaircraft gun—a five-inch, single-barrel weapon being installed on all new ships. Rather than being controlled from the site of the gun, these new weapons were directed electronically, a forerunner to the modern computer. Part of our job was to understand the electric-hydraulic system, how to calibrate and adjust it, and how to diagnose and correct malfunctions.

Morena's pregnancy and the uncertainty over my future left her in an anxious state. Then everything changed. Near the end of my course, the instructional department head called me into his office. Instead of sending me back into combat, he wanted me to join the instructional staff—assuming I passed the final exam with a high mark.

I was happy to pursue this new opportunity. It would mean staying with Morena and our new child, as well as increasing my odds of staying alive for the next few years. I scored high enough on the exam to suit the department head. I was assigned to the gunner's mate school as an instructor.

Because of the war and the demand for qualified navy personnel, we needed to graduate twelve hundred students per term. But we had classroom facilities for only four hundred. The result was that the school offered classes around the clock. I was given the graveyard shift, 12:30 a.m. to 7:30 a.m. That was a tough one. When I got home on Friday mornings, I slept a few hours, then joined Morena in weekend activities. My sleep schedule was so fouled up that when it was time for me to teach again early Monday morning, I felt like going to bed instead.

Fortunately, I enjoyed teaching. I already had experience leading Bible studies and found it translated well to my new duties. I took my responsibilities as instructor seriously and tried to reserve enough energy so that I was sharp for class. It was a challenge for all of us. If a student got sleepy, he would stand until he was awake again. After the fifth period, which ended at 5:05 a.m., each student usually cradled his head on his desk for a ten-minute nap. But I had no problem motivating my students. For them, mastering the material might make the difference in combat between life and death.

Our apartment was in the northwest area of Washington. Every evening I rode a streetcar into downtown, getting off at Seventh and Pennsylvania, only a few blocks from both the White House and the Capitol building. I walked across the street to the front of FBI headquarters, then caught a bus to the naval gun factory and my school.

On my trips to the school and back, I noticed hundreds of servicemen walking the streets. Many were from the embarkation station at Fort Meade, on their last visit before being shipped overseas. They would be in combat in the trenches of Europe within ten days. Though the United Service Organization (USO) and similar groups provided entertainment and other support for servicemen in the area, no one appeared to be meeting their spiritual needs. I felt it was critical to get Jesus' gospel message to these men before they faced the enemy. But how could we do it?

Just a few yards from the spot where I got off the streetcar sat the historic Central Union Mission. The social service agency's facility consisted of two seven-story buildings joined in a giant V. The north building served as a temporary emergency home for children, while the south building provided overnight lodging for servicemen for twenty-five cents a night. Though the lodging included some food and space for a reading room, there were no scheduled activities and no spiritual nourishment for the men.

I began to get an idea. The more I looked over the mission, the more I felt it would be ideal for what I had in mind. I met with the mission board's executive committee, explaining my vision and answering questions for two hours. They said they would take it up with the full mission board. Four friends joined me in praying for a positive result.

Later, I met again with the committee. They told me the board heartily endorsed my plan and would turn over the buildings and staff to me with no restrictions.

It was a high point in my Christian life. In my previous ministries, I had always shared responsibility. Now I had a direct assignment from God and was responsible to him alone. Fortunately, *I* was not alone. The four men who'd been praying with me agreed to be on the team to make the vision happen.

Our first target was the servicemen who stayed overnight at the mission. As they got off the elevator each morning, we invited them into the auditorium for coffee and doughnuts. We then invited them to stay for gospel services, at 9:30 for the early risers and at 11:00 for those who slept longer.

A number of the fellows went out and invited men off the streets. We used the Downing family's well-traveled Chevy to invite and transport men from more remote areas. It didn't take long to fill up the car, drop men off at the mission, and go back again for more. Every meeting at the mission was well attended.

The response to our talks about Jesus was even more gratifying. After every service, several men would indicate their desire to commit their lives to Christ. We followed up by giving them Bible verses to memorize. For months, nearly every mail delivery brought requests from our former guests. Most came from the front lines in Europe. It was exciting to be making a difference in the lives of these men.

There was more for us to do, however. Thousands of women worked in the Washington area for the army, marines, coast guard, and navy during the day, then returned to their hotels and apartments for the night. They sometimes ventured into the streets, usually in groups, but appeared to have no organized activities. The USO served only the men. What could we do to support these women spiritually?

The solution required a giant leap of faith. I visited a realtor and learned of a house near our apartment that was about to go on the market. It had four bedrooms, an attic, a basement, and close access to a main bus line and streetcar. The house would be perfect as a base for a women's ministry, as well as a new home for Morena and me.

Housing was scarce, so I knew the realtor would be flooded with offers as soon as the home was listed. I said a brief prayer and signed a lease on the spot.

Shortly after signing the lease, I received a phone call from the owner of the real estate company. Another agent had promised the house to someone and they wanted me to break the lease. But I believed God had provided this home for our work, so I refused. The monthly $120 payments, along with other expenses, far exceeded our budget. Fortunately, those involved in our ministry gave generously to make up the difference.

Morena led the ministry that we started there, which included Bible studies and prayer meetings, most often at the house. She did a great job. More than fifty years later, we were still receiving letters from some of the women who participated.

I admired Morena for managing both the ministry and her pregnancy. The time inevitably came, however, when her pregnancy claimed first priority. On February 8, 1944, Morena went into labor.

In those days, hospitals were overcrowded. When the moment of delivery approached, the doctor would phone all the hospitals until he found a vacancy, then call the anxious mother. We were fortunate to have a working phone in our new home. We'd been put on a waiting list, with no prospect of having the phone connected during the war. One day, however, the disconnected phone rang. It was the phone company. The man on the line said the White House told them we needed a phone connected. And while everyone we knew had a party line, we were given a private line. Later, I discovered the explanation for this first-class treatment—a friend's brother was chief of protocol at the White House.

Eventually the doctor called and directed us to Providence Hospital. Poor Morena spent twenty-six hours in labor before our breech baby, Marobeth (a combination of the names *Mary* and *Bethany*), was born on February 9. After delivery there was no room available, so Morena's bed was rolled into the hallway, which is where I first visited her.

I was still in the hall when a nurse brought Marobeth out of the nursery to Morena for the first time. When the nurse saw me, she gave me a dressing down I will never forget. She let me know that I was covered with filthy germs, I had no respect for life, and I had probably infected every baby in the hospital. I imagined this was a preview of what a sinner would feel like in heaven.

A few months later, Marobeth accompanied Morena and me to New York. Through our ministry, I'd met the youth evangelist Jack Wyrtzen. Jack was putting on a huge youth rally at Madison Square Garden and had invited me to tell the story of my journey to Jesus. I walked onstage in front of an overflowing crowd of more than twenty-five thousand people and a television audience, certainly the biggest group I'd ever addressed. I was a little nervous, but fortunately my speech was typed out on paper and the bright lights made it impossible to see more than a few rows of people. I'm not sure how good a job I did, but the huge audience gave me a nice ovation.

Our ministry in Washington, D.C., continued to thrive and expand—as did our family. Our second child, Jonathan—another breech baby—was born April 6, 1945, at the Columbia Hospital for Women. A nurse put a sailor hat on him. When I first saw his square jaw, he reminded me of the prizefighter Jack Dempsey. He was so handsome that the nurses started flirting with him.

★　★　★

America's armies and navies seemed to be thriving as well. Throughout 1943, our troops made steady advances in the Solomon Islands. On June 6, 1944, the Allies launched the massive D-Day landing on the northern coast of France. Two months later, Paris was liberated from Nazi rule. In October 1944, the US Navy scored a decisive victory against Japan in the Battle of Leyte Gulf in the Philippines. The cost in lives was appalling, but it began to seem as if victory was on the horizon.

At the gunner's mate school, I had been named department head of small- and medium-caliber guns instruction, a position that technically required an officer's rank. One day the officer in charge decided to correct the situation. He called me into his office and quickly got to the point: "Do you want to be an ensign or a warrant officer?"

"I don't recall expressing any desire for either," I said.

"How old are you?"

"Thirty-one."

"That will be ensign," he said. Ensign was a higher rank than warrant officer. The officer in charge apparently believed that my age and experience merited the extra promotion.

I passed a written exam and was then interviewed by a navy captain. The interview was short. "Who works the hardest," he asked, "enlisted men or commissioned officers?"

I had my doubts but responded, "Officers." It was the answer the captain was looking for. I found out during the next eleven years that I'd guessed correctly.

On February 15, 1945, I was sworn in as a navy ensign. One of the biggest adjustments to my new status was the constant motion of my right arm. Every time I walked out of my classroom building, I had to return the salutes of dozens of men from the various schools.

This problem was nearly solved for me when I received orders to report to the gunnery department on the battleship *South Dakota*, which was heavily involved in the Pacific war. The news was a shock. We had roots and a good ministry going in Washington. Morena and I prayed about it, asking if this was truly the Lord's will. We got our answer when my officer in charge heard about it and made some phone calls. The transfer orders were canceled.

I received another shock on April 12. Franklin Delano Roosevelt, the man who had led our nation in peacetime and war for twelve years, suffered a massive cerebral hemorrhage in Warm Springs, Georgia. Our president was dead. Few men in history had been assigned so much responsibility and handled it so well. I felt he'd been appointed by God to serve our country during this critical time.

I was on duty the night the president's death was announced

over the radio. At the first class break, I reported the news over the public address system. Instead of the usual loud talking in the halls during the ten-minute break, there was silence and grieving.

When my shift ended after midnight, I drove past the White House on my way home. Although the president's body had not yet arrived from Warm Springs, many men and women walked up and down in front of the iron fence on Pennsylvania Avenue. On April 14, I was among the servicemen who formed a corridor for the funeral procession from Union Station to the White House, part of a crowd of three hundred thousand people. I commanded a company of sailors that lined the street north of the Capitol building. I saluted as the caisson and riderless horse passed.

I had very different feelings two weeks later when another death was announced. With Allied troops closing in, Adolf Hitler, instigator of world war, leader of Germany and the purported Thousand-Year Third Reich, took his own life in a Berlin bunker. The Nazi empire and the evil that formed it had finally collapsed. Germany officially surrendered on May 8.

By August, Germany's partner in war also found itself in a difficult position. The Philippines had been liberated from Japan, and the United States held the island of Okinawa, less than a thousand miles from Tokyo. But the Japanese showed no sign of giving up. In June, Prime Minister Kantaro Suzuki had announced that Japan would fight to the end rather than accept unconditional surrender.

America now possessed a weapon, however, that was capable of ending the war quickly—a weapon that would take humanity into a new and even more dangerous age. Since 1942, thousands of American scientists had worked on the secret Manhattan Project to develop an atomic bomb. We were in a race against the Germans to create this deadly weapon, with the fate of the world in the balance. In July 1945, American scientists in New Mexico conducted the first successful test of the bomb.

President Harry Truman determined that a prolonged invasion of Japan would cost hundreds of thousands of lives. The only way to stop the war now was with the new weapon. On August 6, a B-29 bomber—the "Enola Gay"—dropped an A-bomb on the Japanese city of Hiroshima, killing eighty thousand people instantly. Three days later, we dropped a second A-bomb on Nagasaki, causing the deaths of about forty thousand more. In the months following the bombings, thousands more Japanese people died from radiation poisoning and other related effects.

The cost in lives was terrible, but I believe President Truman made the right decision. The Japanese had fortified their beaches with concrete barriers. An invasion of Japan would have been more devastating for both Japan and America. The bombings were the lesser of two evils.

Just a few days after the A-bombs dropped, my officer in charge asked me to teach a one-hour class on the atomic bomb, the "weapon of the future." The limitations were unusual—I wasn't allowed to use notes, and the students were not allowed to take notes. I knew little about the subject, so I was granted top secret clearance and given access to records at what became the Atomic Energy Commission. (I didn't know then that I would gain firsthand knowledge of this lethal weapon a few years hence.)

I was on duty the night of August 14 (August 15 in Japan) when I received the news that Japan had surrendered. At the first coffee break, I made the announcement over the public address system. The navy students were overjoyed, so much so that I couldn't get them back into class. Why study if the war was over? I kept them in the building, but I soon gave up trying to get the students to return to class. I was ready to celebrate with them.

At last, the long conflict had ended. My strongest emotions were gratitude and a sense of relief. I had survived the war and could begin to make plans for the future again. Would I stay in the navy? Would we have more children? How could we best serve the Lord? I was a different man from the one who left Plevna in 1932, with different goals and greater responsibilities. My primary mission was no longer to please myself by pursuing a life of politics and the presidency, but to please my maker.

God had not forgotten my old dream, however. A couple of months after Japan's surrender, Jack Wyrtzen and Dawson Trotman were the lead speakers for a Navigator conference in Washington. One of the attendees was the chief of the White House Secret Service. He offered to give us a tour of his workplace.

After midnight on the Sunday night after the conference, we made our way through a snowstorm to the White House. Morena was with us. Our host seemed to show us everything except the president's living quarters, since President Truman had retired for the night. We sat in the Cabinet Room for a mock high-level meeting. I was tempted to take a souvenir, a pad with notes scribbled by Secretary of the Navy James

Forrestal. We also toured the Oval Office. Along with each of the others, I took my turn sitting at President Truman's desk.

Behind me were the famous three sets of windowpanes, the curtains now drawn. To my left against the wall was a glass case containing a number of the trinkets that used to cover the desk of President Roosevelt—the one I still remember was a miniature US flag in a stand. The top of President Truman's desk was bare compared to his predecessor's, but it did include a recently acquired plaque that read, "The Buck Stops Here!"

The Lord had remembered my ambitions after all, and in his own way put me in the White House. I had to agree that even though I'd taken on many new obligations during the past four years—husband, wartime sailor, instructor, officer, ministry leader, and father—my responsibilities could not equate with those of the man who sat at this desk. I hoped that God would guide and bless the real president in the same way I felt God was guiding and blessing me.

★ 10 ★

FROM HOT TO COLD

THE WORLD WAR WAS OVER, but a new and different battle was just starting. Two superpowers remained at the conclusion of World War II, the United States and the Soviet Union. Our society was founded on freedom—a capitalistic economic system, leaders chosen by the people, a free press, freedom of expression, and freedom to worship. The Soviet state featured socialism and a single-party government that mostly discouraged religious faith and controlled the economy, the press, and to a great extent the lives of its people. Perhaps conflict was inevitable. The Cold War was about to begin.

Initially, though, I did not expect to play a role in America's future conflicts, on or off the battlefield. By the first months of 1946, I'd served in the navy for thirteen-and-a-half years.

Morena and I felt we'd endured enough uncertainty and stress in our four shared years of military life. We decided I should end my navy career and look to the Lord for the next step. I wrote a letter resigning my commission and requesting discharge.

But the Lord had other plans.

In October 1945, Venezuela's military ousted the country's dictator and established a democratic government. The new leadership wanted to rejuvenate its modest fleet and requested America's help. I was asked to help the Venezuelan fleet maintain their guns and keep them battle-ready.

Navy custom was that once you asked to resign, you couldn't change your mind. But when I explained that I'd already submitted a letter of resignation, I was told that the letter could be torn up.

I had prayed before writing that letter, asking God to show me if he wanted me to stay in the navy. I believed the Venezuela position was a clear and remarkable sign of his intervention. I canceled my request for discharge and took a crash course in Spanish. But the assignment didn't materialize. After another change in government personnel, Venezuela's leadership did not pursue the request for American assistance.

My resignation letter was already in the trash. I did not know what would happen next. Soon, however, a similar opportunity arose. The Brazilian navy asked for US help with maintaining and modernizing their equipment, as well as setting up a medical and supply system. I was chosen to be their gunnery expert. I shifted my language study from Spanish to Portuguese.

I traveled to Rio de Janeiro and was taken to a luxurious residence on Copacabana Beach. My assignment turned out to be mostly frustrating, however. Though I made several appointments with the Brazilian fleet's gunnery officer, he didn't keep them. With the war over, Brazil's military men were back to a life of leisure, and we never met. Meanwhile, our military was having trouble arranging transportation for my family. After just six weeks in Brazil, our three-man American contingent received a message from Washington—the base at Rio was to be decommissioned. It was almost a relief.

New orders arrived. I joined the USS *San Carlos*, a seaplane tender based at San Juan, Puerto Rico, as gunnery and communications officer. Morena and the children had yet to make their way to the island when I took a walk through a San Juan park on Sunday morning, August 4, 1946. Suddenly the ground began to shake so violently that I was thrown to the ground. While being tossed around, I crawled to a concrete bench, lay on my stomach on top of it, and wrapped my arms around the bench. The motion continued until I felt like I was seasick.

A local man crawled over and tried to imitate me, but he was so busy crossing himself that he never got a grip on the bench. After the shaking stopped, he noted my uniform and asked, "Did you do that?"

The 8.1-magnitude earthquake was centered on the coast of the Dominican Republic, some 250 miles to the west of us. It hit that country and Haiti hard. Between the quake and tsunamis it created, more than 2,500 people lost their lives in the Caribbean. Thousands more were left homeless.

The Dominican Republic was a closed country about which the world knew little. Nevertheless, that evening the captain had my shipmates and me load the San Carlos with food and medical supplies. The people there needed help. (Of course, a relief mission was also an opportunity to gather intelligence.) We got underway late in the evening and came in sight of the Dominican coast the next morning. The captain called me to the bridge. "Mr. Downing," he said, "you are in charge of the landing party."

Since we didn't know how deep the water was, the captain didn't want the ship too close to shore. The captain and I, along with other members of the crew, searched our charts for a place to land. Through binoculars, we spotted a speck of white that might have been a beach. There were people moving about on shore.

I didn't know how hospitable our reception on the beach might be. "Captain," I said, "I recommend that the landing party be armed with rifles and side arms."

In a loud voice meant for all within earshot, the captain answered, "Mr. Downing, you know you can't land an armed force in another country. It could create an international incident."

Chastened, I left the bridge. The captain followed and whispered in my ear, "That boat is United States property, and you are a United States citizen. You are the gunnery officer. Take whatever arms you need to protect yourselves and the US property in your custody."

I was learning that for some leaders, deniability was part of the game.

My team boarded a twenty-two-foot motor whaleboat. Our party consisted of a doctor, a hospital corpsman, an interpreter/intelligence officer, and the boat crew. The officer was a lieutenant and I was an ensign, so he outranked me. But I'd been appointed to lead the mission, so I was in charge. We wore life jackets and carried rifles and .45-caliber pistols.

As we approached land, dozens of natives headed for the beach. Some were in military uniforms and carried rifles. We couldn't tell if they were friendly or not.

As the water grew shallow, I noticed a series of sharp rocks. I was afraid we would hit one and tear a hole in the boat, so I ordered the coxswain to back away and drop anchor. We were more than a hundred yards from shore. "We'll have to swim the rest of the way," I said.

My team didn't believe this was the most brilliant idea they'd ever heard. One said what the others were probably thinking: "We don't want to do this."

But I'd been ordered to land, and land I would. Fully clothed and armed only with a pistol, I jumped over the side. "Follow me," I said. The others reluctantly joined me in the water.

Fortunately, our weapons were unnecessary. When we reached the beach we were greeted with cheers by the crowd of more than two hundred. Even the armed soldiers welcomed us.

Four of us spent two or three hours surveying the situation and determining what food and medical supplies to offer. The greatest need was for bandages. Many of the injured had open wounds covered by green leaves, already dried out and stuck in the wounds. We unloaded our supplies at a nearby landing over several boat trips, and then, our mission accomplished, we headed back to San Juan.

I was relieved to be back. I'd been afraid that the Dominican dictator, Rafael Trujillo, would find out about our mission and send his soldiers. Then I really would have been responsible for an international incident.

Morena and the children finally arrived in San Juan from New York, where they'd been staying with friends. The first shock they received was the difference in temperature, as the high each day rose past eighty degrees. But it was San Juan's extreme poverty that left the most lasting impression.

Our maid lived on the waterfront, where thousands of families had erected shacks on stilts. Morena drove her home one day and saw that the only decorations on the wall of our maid's shack were Christmas cards she'd retrieved from our wastebasket. When the tide came in, the shack had two feet of water beneath it—thus the stilts.

After a year based in San Juan, our family was on the move again. I was assigned as gunnery officer to the *Nespelen*, a tanker capable of carrying 600,000 gallons of aviation gasoline. Morena and I bought our first house, a small, three-bedroom home in Norfolk, Virginia.

One day in the summer of 1948 I was officer of the deck, meaning I was on the bridge and responsible for the navigation and safety of the ship in the absence of the captain. The *Nespelen* was departing New York City. Ambrose Channel, between the Hudson River and the Atlantic Ocean, is about one thousand yards wide and well-marked with buoys. On this day, though, the channel was blanketed in a thick fog, with visibility only about a quarter mile. I was keeping a close watch on the radar when I observed a large ship coming down the channel in our direction.

I'd already been involved in a collision as officer of the deck a few months earlier on the Delaware River. A Coast Guard buoy tender had ignored our signal and cut across our bow. I didn't want to be in the middle of another one. Sure enough, however, the large ship's bearing remained steady and, contrary to where it should have been, on our side of the channel. We were now a half-mile apart and on a collision course.

The captain was with me on the bridge. "What can we do?" he said. "We are on our side of the channel!"

I pointed out that the water was twenty feet deep on the other side of the buoys. Our draft was only eighteen feet, which meant we could change course and have just enough clearance underneath to get out of the ship's way. The captain chose to maintain our legal right and stay in the deep channel.

Our nemesis, a French crew on a merchant marine vessel named the SS *Indo China*, broke through the fog. It looked huge compared to the *Nespelen*—taller, heavier, and half again as long, and headed straight for us.

I made sure the quartermaster wrote down an almost second-by-second account of our actions. In accordance with the rules of the road, we backed down full and sounded a series of blasts on the whistle, all to no avail. With impact imminent, I sounded the collision alarm.

It appeared that our quartermaster's notes would be in vain. I knew how much fuel we carried in our tanks; I expected the ship to explode. Just like at Pearl Harbor, I thought, *Lord, I will see you in a minute*. I didn't want to hit my head on the ceiling on my way up to heaven, so I stepped outside the pilot house.

The *Indo China* never did reduce speed or change course.

Its bow smashed at an angle into our side about two-thirds back. I was probably a hundred feet away. The jarring of the ship and screech of steel against steel were unforgettable. What I remember most, though, was the sight of steel on both our ships flashing red hot. The collision left a huge hole in our side above the waterline.

But the *Nespelen* did not explode. The bow of the *Indo China* missed our tanks by ten feet. It penetrated our chief petty officer's quarters, but the collision alarm had sounded in time for everyone in the area to evacuate. No one was injured.

Rather than meeting Jesus in heaven, I was still living and breathing on planet Earth. Part of me was relieved, another part was disappointed.

You could say my other most memorable assignments on the *Nespelen* were polar opposites from my station on the *San Carlos* in San Juan. Every summer we transported fuel to an air force base in Newfoundland. As we approached the massive, ice-covered island on the first of those trips, the fog was thick, the weather windy, the seas choppy, and the waters poorly charted. We could not find the entrance to the fjord that led to the base, so we dropped anchor for the night. In the morning, the fog cleared and we discovered the source of our troubles. A huge iceberg blocked the entrance. It had showed up on our radar as coastline. As the iceberg moved slowly to sea, we were able to maneuver around it and complete our duties.

By 1950, I had been promoted to lieutenant junior grade. In February, the *Nespelen* was chosen for an unusual mission. The air force wanted to know if we could supply its base on Lake Melville in Labrador, Canada, about 40 degrees latitude from the North Pole. We were tasked with penetrating the ice as far as possible into Lake Melville.

The navy welded a two-inch belt of steel around the ship at the waterline and issued us cold-weather outfits that included face masks. I bought a pair of oversized wool-lined boots to accommodate extra pairs of socks. My initiative backfired, though. Since I was one of the few who could keep my feet from freezing, I felt obligated to volunteer for the prolonged-exposure, below-zero jobs. One of these was standing on deck and watching the fantail to try to keep our propellers from hitting large blocks of ice.

The icepack at Labrador extended forty miles off shore, but with the help of the navy's largest icebreaker and a smaller breaker about the size of our ship, we eventually made it to Lake Melville. We evaluated our capabilities and limitations and declared our monthlong research project complete.

It was to be my last ship assignment for some time. While we were en route to a Newfoundland naval base for repairs, I received new orders. Apparently my teaching skills were back in demand. I was to report to the Merchant Marine Academy at King's Point, New York, as an assistant professor of naval science.

My adventures at sea were not the only excitement experienced by the Downing family in those years. In 1947, while we were in Norfolk, Morena was pregnant with our third child. On September 2, her labor pains were steady. As I tried to hurry her into the car, she noticed clothes on our clothesline and insisted on taking them down before we left.

Getting across the bay from our house to the naval hospital in Portsmouth required a fifteen-minute ferry boat ride. I imagined myself delivering our child in the backyard or while waiting in traffic for the ferry. But we made it onto the first available ferry and to the hospital.

Since Morena's earlier labors had been so long, I returned home and waited an hour before calling the hospital to check on progress. To my surprise, the nurse informed me I was already a father again. We named the new baby Jim.

Our family grew even larger on January 21, 1950. Joe was also born in Portsmouth. Since at that time fathers weren't allowed in the delivery room, I was outside in the waiting area, as usual. Unbeknownst to me, there was tension in the delivery room. I found out from the doctor that Joe was a "blue baby"—something was wrong with his circulation and he couldn't breathe during the delivery. But they solved the problem in time, and Joe never suffered any lasting effects.

Joe's life in Norfolk was brief. In August, five-year-old Jonathan and I drove to New York in the family car, now a 1940 Buick, to look for a home within reasonable distance of my new teaching position. I had told Jonathan about the tall buildings we would see. As we drove through Manhattan, he voiced his amazement: "You didn't say they were *that* tall." We eventually purchased a two-story Cape Cod home on Long Island for $18,000.

Over the next two years, I taught ordnance and gunnery, seamanship, military law and justice, and naval history at the

Merchant Marine Academy. We had no military duties. One semester I was through teaching at 10 a.m. four days a week and had no classes on Wednesdays. Classroom teaching truly is hard work, but even so those two years were undoubtedly the easiest of my naval career. I was promoted to a full-grade lieutenant during this time.

A little more than three months after Joe's birth, we learned that Morena was pregnant again. One of her doctors had a knack for discovering twins and bet another doctor five dollars that Morena was having two babies. They gave her an x-ray to settle the bet. I talked with a nurse just after the film was developed and asked her if it was twins. She said she couldn't disclose the information, but the look on her face betrayed what she knew.

On the last day of January, 1951, I drove Morena to the hospital on slick and snowy roads. Being a veteran mother, Morena gave birth to the twins quickly: Donald and David Downing. When we brought them home a few days later, we had to hire a girl to help us during the day. If you are a parent, you must have as great an appreciation as I still do for Morena's ability to care for six preschoolers, three of them in diapers.

Our family enjoyed exploring New York, interrupted by brief moments of parental terror. My greatest sightseeing scare came on our family visit to the Statue of Liberty. When we were inside, Jon and Jim thought the rest of us were too slow and ran up the steps and out of sight. They went all the way to the crown. I didn't know how high the walls were up there and pictured my boys climbing up a railing and falling over. I was really huffing and puffing when I caught up with them.

The kids' tendency to run ahead wasn't my only concern

at the time. The Cold War was heating up. In June 1948, the Soviet Union blocked railway, road, and canal access to the Western territories of Berlin, cutting off food and supplies. Western nations responded with an airlift, delivering tons of goods. The blockade continued for eleven months before the Soviets abandoned it in May 1949.

A bigger crisis began a year later. In June 1950, North Korean forces, aided by the Soviet Union and China, invaded South Korea. To counter this move, United Nations forces, led by the United States, moved into South Korea. They repelled the North's advance and soon moved into North Korea. In October, China entered the war and pushed the UN troops back. That was the development that alarmed me and raised tensions across the country. Most Americans were already worried about the Communists and their aim to conquer the world. As the fighting in Korea dragged on, the possibility of escalation into a larger war involving America and the Soviet Union hung over all our heads.

I was tired and sick of war. I resented that after so much fighting around the world, we still hadn't resolved our differences. I was ready for a life of peace.

In many ways, it was our ministry that kept everything in perspective. In Norfolk, we completed a servicemen's center for evangelism and discipleship in the downtown bar district, where we also recruited and trained businessmen to multiply our efforts. In New York, we led a weekly Bible study in our home. I was chairman of the deacon board and Sunday school superintendent at the Conservative Baptist Church nearby. I also taught an evening class at the National Bible Institute in Manhattan.

Perhaps we devoted a little too much time to our ministry. In hindsight, maybe I should have worked harder at being closer to each of my children. Yet so often it was our ministry efforts that gave me energy, a feeling of fulfillment, and a reminder that God was in control regardless of what was going on in the world.

In a sense, we were fighting two wars. One was against Communism and those who sought to take away our freedoms. The other was against the spiritual forces of darkness that aimed to prevent people from knowing and joining up with Jesus. I was only a small cog in an epic battle. My role remained to obey, to serve, and to fight.

★11★

CAPTAIN DOWNING

IN THE SPRING OF 1943, I was bicycling through the Pearl Harbor naval base when I saw a sleek-looking ship with a large number *1* painted on her bow. I admired her appearance as she tied up to a pier and wondered about her purpose. I had not seen one like her before. As I got closer, I saw that she was the USS *Patapsco*. I later learned she was the first of fifteen gasoline tankers in her class to be built during the war.

I never dreamed that less than ten years later I would become her captain.

In the summer of 1952, almost two years to the day after I joined the instructional staff at King's Point, I received new orders. To my surprise, I was given command of the same gasoline tanker I'd admired back at Pearl Harbor. In terms of rank and my brief time served as a lieutenant, I was the junior commanding officer in the Pacific Fleet.

Perhaps it should not have been a total shock. Throughout my tenure as an officer, I'd always scored at least 90 percent on my quarterly fitness reports in the category "eligibility to succeed to command." I did not expect it, but my superiors obviously felt I was ready.

Being given a command was a new level of responsibility and potentially dangerous, especially since we were in the midst of the Korean War. But the *San Carlos* and the *Nespelen* were both similar to the *Patapsco*, so I was familiar with the work and the type of ship. I was confident I was up to the job.

Early in August, I drove the family in the Buick to Little Rock, where they would live until joining me in Honolulu for Christmas. I can hardly believe I drove with little Don on my lap, his hands on the steering wheel—no seatbelts then. I remember David intently watching Morena eat ice cream and uttering his first words: "Me me me."

From Little Rock, I took a train to San Francisco, then flew to Honolulu, Wake Island, and Tokyo. The *Patapsco* was stationed at the navy base at the Japanese port Sasebo.

My new vessel was 310 feet and nine inches long, with a beam (width) of forty-eight feet and six inches. It was powered by four diesel-electric engines with twin screws and armed with four three-inch, .50-caliber air and surface guns, four groups of twenty-millimeter antiaircraft machine guns, and a couple of additional .50-caliber machine guns. The crew was supposed to be a complement of 125, though we usually operated with fewer than one hundred.

On August 22, I participated in the change-of-command ceremony. This included hours of exercises on the water for the new captain to certify that the ship was seaworthy and the crew was trained and ready for war. (Though my rank was lieutenant, in the navy any ship's commander is addressed as captain.) Once the certification was completed, we gathered the crew on deck. I read my orders aloud and saluted the outgoing captain. With the words "I relieve you, sir," I was officially in command.

The day was so packed that it was a week before I remembered it had been my thirty-ninth birthday.

I might have been familiar with the usual duties of a gasoline tanker, but not with my first mission as captain of the *Patapsco*. Since the Korean conflict was primarily a land war, antiaircraft gun crews tended to get rusty. Our job was to meet every United Nations ship traveling in and out of Korea and give them practice shooting at the twenty-some planes we carried.

Our airplanes had twelve-foot wingspans. Forerunners to the drones that today's military employs so frequently in hot spots around the world, these planes were piloted remotely, guided by an onboard naval aviator with a handheld joystick. If our UN allies scored a direct hit, there was nothing to recover. But if the target plane survived, our "pilot" sent a signal that stopped its engine and popped its parachute for a water landing, at which point we would recover it. I acquired more experience in ship handling while recovering those planes than most captains get in their careers.

After three and a half months of this duty, we were ordered to return to Pearl Harbor. I persuaded my operational commander to let us go to Tokyo first. Our diesel engines had not had extensive maintenance for several months; they needed downtime. So did my crew—since many sailors joined the navy to "see the world," I felt a stay in Japan was mandatory for morale purposes. We anchored in Yokohama Bay for a week of R&R (rest and relaxation).

After arrival we discovered that evangelist David Morken was holding nightly services near Yokohama in a huge tent borrowed from Presbyterian missionaries. The local Navigators staff—Roy Robertson, Bob Boardman, and Warren Myers—were assisting. I met with them several times until our week was up, and the crew and I set off on the *Patapsco* for Pearl Harbor. About the time we reached open water, however, we got a priority message: A major typhoon was approaching. We should go back to Yokohama and delay departure for twenty-four hours.

Upon our return, I invited the evangelistic team out to the ship for lunch. They had a problem. The typhoon was approaching Yokohama, and the heavy rain was waterlogging their borrowed tent. If they left the tent up, the wind would rip it to pieces. But if they tried to take it down, the weight of the waterlogged canvas would cause it to collapse, causing significant damage. The tent was worth $4,000; they had no funds to replace it.

The men did the right thing. They called an extended prayer meeting.

As the typhoon approached, the wind speed increased. The weather service gave us hourly position reports, which I plotted on our ocean chart. When I joined the points in the form of a graph, I was astonished: The typhoon was curving back to the sea. Soon it had reversed its course 180 degrees. It spent its fury on the open sea.

No typhoon approaching the Japanese coast had ever been known to reverse its course. The next day I showed Morken the plot and gave him a copy. He and his team accepted it as an act of God. I couldn't argue with him.

Months later, we were stationed in the Philippines when we received orders to deliver a load of fuel to the French in Saigon, Vietnam. Viet Minh communists led by Ho Chi Minh controlled much of the northern part of the country, while the French mostly controlled the south. At the time, the United States supported France's aim to regain control of Vietnam. About a year later, the country would be officially partitioned between the two sides along the seventeenth parallel, another step toward what would become the Vietnam War.

It was a tense mission. My operations officer had originally given me a course covering the shortest distance between Manila and Saigon. When I studied it, I felt it took us too close to the coast of China. Given China's involvement in Korea and the mutual hostility between our nation and the Chinese, I objected and was allowed to choose my own course.

After we reached Vietnam, French authorities assigned us a Vietnamese pilot to take us the twenty miles up the river to Saigon. It was a winding course with many sharp turns. I anticipated an ambush around every curve, so I ordered my crew to man our 20-millimeter guns and told them to be ready to shoot if we were threatened. This made our pilot unhappy, but fortunately our journey turned out to be uneventful. Our only fighting was against the monster mosquitos that invaded our hotel rooms through unscreened open windows.

★ ★ ★

Shemya was a small (three miles by four miles) windswept island near the western end of Alaska's Aleutian Islands chain, closer to Russia than to Alaska's mainland. The air force had recently closed its base there and left shiploads of aviation fuel behind. Our new mission was to transport that fuel to bases at Attu and Adak, other islands in the Aleutians.

The air force had blasted away rocks along Shemya's shore and built a small pier where ships could dock. But storms (called williwaws in Alaska) had broken and washed away two-thirds of the pier.

I studied my charts. My challenge was to dock the Patapsco at a pier that was one-third the ship's length without crashing into the rocks at the shoreline or at the edge of the blasted-out channel. I felt my chances of docking successfully were not good.

I spent a long night thinking about my options. There were only two. Since a navy captain is forbidden to subject his ship to unnecessary hazards, I could refuse the mission. I didn't think that would be the brightest career move.

The other option was to try. Worst case, I would strand the *Patapsco* on the rocks. The navy would invest much time and money to refloat and repair the ship. I would be court-martialed, and would likely be fined and prevented from receiving significant responsibility for the rest of my career. But I could remain in the navy.

Neither option was especially appealing. I decided that I had to try. The next question, then, was how?

The bow of our ship was made of reinforced steel and was pretty tough. I decided to approach the pier at eight knots and bury the bow of the ship in the end of the pier. Members of the crew would secure the bow to the pier. Then we'd put out lines to the stern and haul the ship alongside the pier with mooring lines. I explained my plan to the officers and crew so they would be prepared for the upcoming collision.

The day of our attempt was foggy, so we waited about ten miles offshore until midmorning, when the mist lifted. We were about to find out if I still had a career in the navy.

We went in. I told the helmsman to aim for the end of the pier. As we approached, I backed down the engines to reduce our speed. "Stand by for collision!" I announced over the ship's loudspeaker.

Just then, the wind picked up. I was alarmed to see we were being pushed to the left. It appeared we might miss the pier altogether and slam into the rocks.

Instead, however, we missed the rocks by several feet, and glided alongside the pier right into our berth. It was the best landing I ever made. My career was saved.

I was sorry I'd announced my plan to the crew ahead of time. If I hadn't, they would have thought me a master at docking.

I was ready to put my career on the line in another incident during our time in the Aleutians. I'd already heard that in the Mediterranean, unidentified ships that I was sure were Russian sometimes played "chicken" with our ships. One of their ships would head straight for one of our vessels and try to move it off course. The Russians also sometimes "joined" our aircraft-carrier task forces, operating as though they were part of the formation. In a time of nearly open hostility, they were testing our resolve.

Unidentified vessels operated in international waters off Alaska as well. One night our radar picked up a vessel headed directly toward us at about forty knots (approximately forty-six miles per hour). The heading had to have been deliberate. I was pretty certain it was a torpedo boat from another nation's navy, practicing a torpedo run on us.

The boat approached on our starboard side. Although I had the right of way, they were daring me to yield.

Germany and Japan's actions at the beginning of World War II had already shown me what happens when one nation acts aggressively and the other fails to respond. I would not be the "chicken" who backed down against the unknown vessel. I sounded general quarters—all hands to their battle stations.

"When she gets within a mile of us," I told my officers, "we'll fire a warning shot with our three-inch .50 caliber gun."

The unidentified vessel closed within two miles of us, then a mile and a half. We did not change course. Neither did the other ship. Finally, just before the distance closed to a critical distance, the other vessel veered off. No shots were fired. I canceled general quarters.

Later, after we reached our base in Anchorage, some of the crew talked about how we'd "almost started a war." The news reached the ears of the operations officer at the Alaskan Sea Frontier command. He called me in for a chat.

"You can't fire on another nation like that," he told me. "It will cause an international incident."

I wasn't going to back down that easily. "I was at Pearl Harbor," I said. "I saw our weakness there. Weakness invites aggression. What you should do the next time that happens is send us air cover. That will send them a message."

I don't think the officer took me seriously. He just wanted to avoid an incident that might escalate the Cold War. Once again, I was learning a lesson.

By midyear 1953, forces in Korea had battled to a virtual stalemate, with the opposing armies roughly divided along the thirty-eight parallel. Peace negotiations that had dragged on for two years were finally completed. On July 27, 1953, representatives of the United Nations, North Korea, and China signed an armistice. The Korean conflict was over. But the Cold War and the struggle for global domination were not.

★ ★ ★

In 1953, Mitsuo Fuchida, the commander who had led Japan's surprise attack on Pearl Harbor, returned to the scene of his former glory. The *Patapsco* was stationed there at the time. A Christian group was hosting a reception for Fuchida on the other side of the island and invited Morena and me to attend.

Fuchida was now fifty. He had recently converted to Christianity. He was slim and much shorter than I, wearing a suit and tie with his hair neatly trimmed. As Morena and I waited in the line to greet him, my emotions bounced between extremes, not unlike the day the bombs fell so many years before. What right did this man have to come here after what he'd done to so many American heroes? Why was I here?

Yet the war was part of his past, not his future. We were both on God's side now.

Fuchida was nearly killed three times during World War II. The first incident was a crash landing on Borneo during the Battle of Java, which killed a crewmate. The second was during the Battle of Midway, when a bomb struck the carrier *Akagi* and blew Fuchida into the ocean. The *Akagi* sank and Fuchida's ankles were broken, but he was rescued. The third incident was when we dropped the A-bomb on Hiroshima on August 6, 1945. Fuchida had been in the city since August 3 and had planned to stay until August 6, but he agreed to a last-minute request to assist another officer in another city and left the afternoon before. After the war, Fuchida retired to become a farmer. He was bitter and disillusioned about how the war and his life had turned out, but as the years passed, he began to wonder about his mysterious survival during the war.

Fuchida credited his survival to a great, unseen power. Then one day in Tokyo near the end of 1949, an American missionary handed him a leaflet that told the story of Sergeant Jacob DeShazer, a crewman aboard one of the Doolittle Raid planes. Just after the raid, DeShazer's bomber had run out of fuel over China. He parachuted and was captured by the Japanese. He was tortured by his captors, intensifying his hatred of them. But over several quiet nights, DeShazer began to think about his old Sunday school lessons. He asked for a Bible and soon surrendered his heart to Jesus. Over time he changed his attitude toward his guards, and eventually became a missionary in Japan.

Fuchida was moved by DeShazer's story and bought a New Testament for himself. He read until he came to the scene of Jesus' crucifixion and his words in verse Luke 23:34: "Father, forgive them; for they know not what they do."

Fuchida realized that he was one of "them." For forty-seven years, he had not known what he was doing. He now understood that Christ had died for his sin. He wrote, "Now, I receive the only Son of God, Jesus Christ, as my Savior."

Our turn came to greet Fuchida. Morena put out her hand and shook his. "Isn't it wonderful," she said, "that although we were enemies, now we are brothers and sisters in Christ?" He nodded and smiled.

I was next. I couldn't bring myself to do it, could not join in that warm welcome. I had seen too many friends die.

My right arm stayed at my side. I looked Fuchida in the eye and said, "I was on the *West Virginia* during the attack."

"Yes," he said, and nodded at me. "I remember that ship."

In the group discussion that followed, I watched and listened closely to our visitor from Japan. I detected no pride in what he'd done during the war. He struck me instead as humble and genuinely repentant. A few years later, he overnighted several times at Glen Eyrie, the Navigator headquarters, on his travels through Colorado Springs. I greeted him there multiple times. Since his English was poor and I did not speak Japanese, I never tried to engage him in deep conversation. When I read some of his writings, though, I felt even more convinced that his spiritual conversion was real. He was sorry for his previous actions. Like so many, he'd been led astray by others in authority.

Jesus forgave his killers, and he calls upon Christians to forgive those who wrong us. For my part, I can say now that in my heart I have forgiven Mitsuo Fuchida for his role in the Pearl Harbor attack. I cannot yet say the same about the Japanese leaders who stirred up so much ambition and hate. I am not a perfect Christian. After eighty-plus years in the faith, I'm still working on it.

★12★

CASTLE BRAVO

THE ATOMIC BOMBS DROPPED on Hiroshima and Nagasaki ended World War II and ushered in the era of weapons of mass destruction. Our leaders and scientists were determined to stay ahead of Joseph Stalin and the Soviet scientists, who were developing their own nuclear weapons.

The US effort, named Operations Crossroads, had a budget of $1.3 billion. The plan was to conduct three atomic bomb tests to determine their effectiveness. The bomb in the first test, Able, would be released in the air, while the Baker bomb would be detonated underwater. (Charlie, the third scheduled bomb test, was later canceled.)

For the test site, the navy chose Bikini Atoll, a ring of small islands in the Marshall Islands. Bikini, another Pacific paradise where white sand beaches circled sparkling lagoons, was

2,700 miles southwest of Hawaii and relatively unpopulated. The navy convinced the 167 natives on Bikini to temporarily relocate to another island. They were told they'd be returned in a few months.

On July 1, 1946, the Able bomb was loaded onto a B-29 Superfortress bomber nicknamed *Dave's Dream*. When the plane took off, an excited radio commentator exclaimed, "The atom bomb is in the air and on its way to Bikini for the greatest experiment in history." Just before 9 a.m., the bomb was released, exploding 518 feet above a Bikini lagoon. A ball of fire erupted into the air, reaching a temperature of 100,000 degrees Fahrenheit—hotter than the surface of the sun.

Purple, red, and white clouds swirled above the lagoon. An already familiar mushroom-shaped cloud rose forty thousand feet into the sky. The test was a success. (That same year, a French fashion designer created a new two-piece bathing suit for women and named it the bikini, describing it as "like the bomb . . . small and devastating.")

The second test, Baker, was conducted on July 25. The bomb exploded underwater, generating a shock wave that dug a crater two hundred feet below the ocean floor. One second after the explosion, an expanding fireball threw more than two million tons of water, sand, and pulverized coral more than a mile high. The explosion also created tsunami-like waves.

The yield of the bomb dropped on Hiroshima was sixteen kilotons (16,000 tons) of TNT; the Nagasaki bomb was twenty-one kilotons. Each of the bombs exploded at Bikini had a yield the equivalent of twenty-three kilotons. The Bikini bombs were the most powerful ever detonated.

America was not alone in its A-bomb efforts, however. In 1949, the Soviet Union detonated its first atomic bomb, in Kazakhstan. The yield was twenty kilotons. The race to stay ahead of the Soviets was on.

The United States exploded more atomic bombs in the Marshall Islands: three before the Soviet test, in 1948; four in 1951; and two in 1952. But scientists were turning their focus to a new weapon: the hydrogen bomb. The difference was fission versus fusion. To create an A-bomb explosion, heat was generated by fission, the division of particles of an atom. Fusion bombs operate by fusing atomic particles together, creating a heavier atom and resulting in a much heavier explosion.

The United States conducted its first H-bomb (H meaning "hydrogen") test, codenamed Mike, in 1952. It detonated successfully with a yield of about 11 megatons (11 million tons). But at a weight of eighty-two tons and dimensions bigger than a two-story house, it wasn't practical—no one could load it onto an airplane.

With the help of intelligence delivered by sympathizers within America's nuclear program, the Soviet Union countered the next year with its first H-bomb. It exploded with a yield of four hundred kilotons—less powerful than our Mike, but small enough to be dropped from a plane.

The test sent American scientists and other nuclear officials scrambling. The feeling was that we had to catch up with the Soviets, and quickly, because no one knew what they might do if they felt that they had a weapons advantage.

The A-bomb tests received a great deal of publicity, so I was aware of them. I didn't know a thing about the classified hydrogen bomb efforts, however. I didn't have much time to think about bombs anyway. I was too busy fulfilling my duties aboard the *Patapsco*.

★   ★   ★

In February 1954, the crew and I were on our way to make a routine delivery of liquid cargo to the army at Eniwetok Atoll (now known as Enewetak) in the Marshall Islands. Eniwetok was 190 miles west of Bikini. I expected to spend a few hours there unloading the fuel and then head back to Pearl Harbor.

The journey took seven days. A few weeks before, I'd gone to a Youth for Christ meeting in Honolulu and recognized a member of my crew, Ken Nelson. I barely knew him, but I learned there that Ken was a Christian. After we got underway to Eniwetok, he and a buddy of his joined me in my cabin each night for a Bible study and prayer session. There was just enough space for us—the two of them sat on my bed while I sat in a chair.

Starting at about the fourth night, the tone of the prayers of these two men changed. They began earnestly asking God to provide for the safety of the ship and crew, and for him to give the captain wisdom so that he would do the right thing. After about three nights of these fervent prayers, I began to get annoyed. What was the matter with these guys? Didn't they have confidence in me as their captain? What did they know that I didn't?

I was later ashamed of my annoyance. They didn't possess any special knowledge—they simply sensed the Lord leading them to pray this way. Soon I would discover why.

It was almost sunset on February 25 when we passed Bikini Atoll. I trained my binoculars on the coastline, which was more than a mile away. I didn't know it then, but I was looking at a one-acre, artificial land mass connected to tiny Nam Island. I spotted a tower, probably three to four stories high, with what appeared to be something black hanging from it. I briefly wondered what experiment the government was up to now.

We reached Eniwetok on the morning of February 26 and moored the *Patapsco* near the army ship that was supposed to receive our cargo. During World War I, when steel was in short supply, the United States began constructing ships with concrete hulls. The army was still using one of these at Eniwetok to store fuel. An army representative met with us that afternoon and delivered the surprising news that the concrete ship was leaking. "I'm sorry," he said. "We can't take your fuel."

"Then what am I going to do with our cargo?" I said.

The army representative threw up his hands. "I don't know. The ship is the only storage facility we have."

I was frustrated. We'd come a long way to deliver this fuel, and I intended to complete my mission. The next morning, I had our boat crew take me to a navy destroyer to see the Senior Officer Present Afloat. The SOPA was responsible for making command decisions regarding any ships at Eniwetok.

I was agitated when we spoke. "Calm down," the officer said. "It's lunchtime. Join me and we'll talk it over." Over a meal in the ward room (dining room) on the destroyer—I remember the ship rocked, and I had to hold onto my plate—the SOPA told me about his own frustrations operating in the area with a joint task force consisting of the army, navy, air force, and civilian Atomic Energy Commission. The civilian commission was making all the final decisions, he said.

"I brought this cargo all the way out here, and the army can't receive it," I said. "What am I supposed to do?"

The SOPA, a commander by rank, didn't seem concerned. Then he changed the subject entirely, asking a series of strange questions:

"What kind of protective clothing do you have for the crew?

"Do you have any special washdown equipment?

"What kind of radioactive monitoring instruments do you have on board?"

I found his queries odd, but I answered each. Then he asked, "How fast will your ship go?"

"She can do 13.5 knots (15.5 miles per hour)."

The commander wiped his mouth with his napkin and looked me in the eye. "Captain, I am sworn to secrecy as to the reason," he said. "But if I were in your place, I would get your ship underway and head east at top speed."

I shook my head, thinking there had to be a way to work this out. "I can't leave without orders from my operational commander in Pearl Harbor."

"There isn't time. I'll issue you orders by radio for you to return to Pearl Harbor immediately."

I was flummoxed. My glimpse the night before of the tower on Bikini flashed through my mind, but I dismissed it. Clearly something was going on, but I was sure the SOPA was just being overly cautious.

It appeared I would be taking my cargo back to Pearl. The

boat crew took me back to the *Patapsco,* and we got underway immediately. We passed Bikini near sunrise the next morning, February 28. I again used my binoculars in the dim light to observe the tower near Nam. Nothing looked different from three days before.

The sea was extremely rough, which slowed our progress. Our pace slowed even more when we discovered a broken engine liner—we had to shut down two of our four diesel engines.

Around midnight I received a coded radio message. Since I was the only officer on board authorized to decode the message, I retired to my cabin to translate it. The message was a warning. It advised us to get out of the area at all possible speed and proceed to a specific "safe" zone identified by latitude and longitude. Something big was about to happen, but I didn't know what.

We were already moving toward the safe zone as fast as we could go, though that was only about nine knots (ten miles per hour). There was little else I could do about the coded warning. I stayed up through the rough night, waiting and watching, until fatigue finally set in. At 6 a.m., as daybreak approached, we were nearly 190 miles east of Bikini. I decided to go down to my cabin for a nap. I told the officer of the deck to notify me if anything unusual happened.

About forty-five minutes later, when I had just started to slumber, I heard a knock on my door. It was a messenger. "Captain," he said, "the OOD requests that you come to the bridge."

On the bridge, the officer of the deck said, "Captain, it's faded now, but a few minutes ago all the bridge personnel saw an extremely brilliant light to the west."

I checked the quartermaster's log. Alongside his entry he'd drawn the image of a mushroom, the symbol of an atomic explosion.

Now I began to understand.

The United States had indeed detonated a bomb. Code-named Castle Bravo, it was the first test of a deliverable hydrogen bomb, and it was top secret. President Eisenhower had put the Atomic Energy Commission in charge of the effort and practically ordered the army, navy, and air force to muzzle their public-information officers. He'd threatened that if any military department originated a press release before or after the test, "heads would roll."

I didn't know about any of that then. I also didn't know that our nuclear brain trust had miscalculated. The Bravo bomb was predicted to explode with a yield equivalent to six megatons of TNT. Scientists had included the isotope lithium-7 in the bomb and expected it to be inert at the time of the explosion. They were wrong. Instead, the reaction of lithium-7 with the other elements present produced an explosion two and a half times greater than anticipated—fifteen megatons, at the time the greatest bomb yield ever and still the most powerful ever detonated by the United States. The bomb was about a thousand times more powerful than each of the A-bombs dropped on Hiroshima and Nagasaki.

Castle Bravo created a fireball nearly four miles wide, vaporizing part of Nam. It dug a crater 250 feet deep and more than a mile wide, and sent a mushroom cloud nearly twenty-five miles into the sky.

John Halderman, a Marine corporal, was among those

aboard the USS *Curtiss*, twenty-three miles away, when the bomb was detonated. He had turned away from Ground Zero just before the blast. "We had dark goggles on," he said, "but when it went off, you could see the bone in your arm. It was like looking at an x-ray."

The experts also miscalculated on the weather. They believed that a west wind would blow most of the bomb's fallout toward empty ocean. The wind did blow west—at lower altitudes. But at higher elevations, where most of the radioactive fallout went, the wind blew hard to the east, toward inhabited islands—and my ship.

We continued as best we could through the rough seas toward Honolulu. Sometime that day, we used the conventional Geiger counter on board to check radiation levels. None of the readings appeared unusual, so we put it away.

About 5:30 p.m., a navy plane began circling us, trying to contact us with its searchlight. But there were so many clouds that we couldn't read the message. We finally received the message by radio—we were instructed to not get within four hundred miles of Bikini. It was an appropriate warning but not much help. We were still just 325 miles east of Bikini, increasing the distance as fast as we could. We arrived at Pearl Harbor more than a week after we left Eniwetok.

We were ordered to tie up at Hickham air force base and discharge our well-traveled fuel. Shortly after docking, I received a phone call from my operation commander. He said he'd received word from the Atomic Energy Commission that the *Patapsco* may have been contaminated by radioactive fallout. "Why," he said, "would they think that?"

"Commander," I said, "if you saw the sun rise in the west instead of the east, what would you think?"

"I think we shouldn't talk about this over an unsecured telephone," the commander answered. I went to the commander's office and gave a full report.

In the meantime, the crew resumed normal routine. Those with wives and families, me included, went home for the night. After discharging our fuel the next day, we moved the *Patapsco* to its regular berth at "How" (H) dock.

I was on board when navy yard technicians drove up in a station wagon. They carried instruments and wore white suits and headgear that completely enclosed their bodies. These men turned on their instruments while they were still on the pier. A brisk wind blew in from the sea, across the ship, and toward the pier. As soon as the technicians read the level of radiation in that wind, they ducked behind a shelter. After a few minutes, they jumped back in the station wagon and sped off to safety.

The ship was heavily contaminated. We'd been living with that radiation for more than a week. The government later estimated that we received a rem (roentgen equivalent man) dose of 4.7 during our trip back to Pearl Harbor, roughly equivalent to 470 dental x-rays over the entire body.

We were ordered off the ship immediately and herded together in the shipyard. No one was allowed to leave until he had produced a gallon of urine for testing at a lab in California. I later learned that some people were bumped from their flight so the plane could accommodate our waste and still make its weight limit. Our urine took priority over passengers.

The *Patapsco* was towed to the navy yard for a three-week

washdown with hot water and Tide. No one, including the captain, was allowed access to the ship until the washdown was completed. Meanwhile, the crew and I underwent complete physical examinations. We all had below-normal numbers of white blood cells and abnormally high counts of red blood cells.

Upon arrival at Pearl, we had sent our laundry ashore to be washed. I had the returned laundry checked; it was highly radioactive. I feared we had contaminated all of the laundry service's customers. The crew and I ended up putting all of our clothing, shoes, and bedsheets into steel barrels and then filled the barrels with concrete. These were taken out to sea and dumped into one thousand fathoms of water.

I took a Geiger counter home. There was a radioactive trail every place I'd walked, as well as in my car. My friends treated me like a leper; they refused to shake my hand.

But I had a more immediate problem. I was commanding officer of a US Navy ship. As such, I was required to keep a twenty-four-hour log, take daily power magazine temperatures, rotate the propellers daily, and much more. But I was not allowed on board the ship. And because of the secrecy blanket over the bomb test, I could not put an explanation in writing.

I saw trouble ahead. Overheated ammunition on the ship might explode. At the next inspection, the ship's records would be blank. I could be court-martialed without being allowed to explain.

Vice Admiral Burton Biggs advised me to see the Pacific Fleet public relations officer, Captain William Lederer. In four years, Lederer would coauthor *The Ugly American*, a novel about failings of the US diplomatic corps. The book would become a bestseller and one of the most politically influential novels in American literature. I met Lederer in his office. He was an interesting character. He'd overcome a youthful tendency toward stammering, but he still used it as a tactic in conversation—when he talked and thought I wasn't listening closely, he started to stammer to regain my attention.

When I explained my situation, he saw an opportunity not only to help me with my problem, but also to get a major scoop. He decided to issue a press release, effectively declassifying the operation, so that I could reference it in explaining my inability to fulfill my responsibilities as captain of the *Patapsco*. Lederer drafted a release, checked it with me, and sent it out on the evening of March 23:

> The Navy tanker Patapsco received slight and not dangerous contamination by radioactive fallout during tests in the Eniwetok-Bikini area.
>
> As an extreme precaution, the ship was brought to the Pearl Harbor naval shipyard for checking and complete decontamination.
>
> No personnel received sufficient radiation to be in any way harmful.
>
> Although it has been established that no apparent possibility of injury to crewmembers exists, all members of the crew were removed from the ship and given thorough medical examinations as an extra safety measure.
>
> This examination gave no evidence of any harmful effects from the slight exposure. . . .

Lt. Downing, reached by telephone at his home, said he could add nothing to the release for security reasons without permission. The navy said no permission was in sight.

Obviously, this assessment of the bomb's impact was a cautious one. At least one congressman, Rep. Chet Holifield of California, was far less cautious in his own comments that week: The explosion, he said, "was so far beyond what was predicted that you might say it was out of control."

Lederer's press release made front-page headlines in Honolulu and across the country. Some stories included a photo of me and description of my family background. I began getting calls and notes from people I hadn't heard from in years. But Lederer's efforts solved my problem. The secret was out.

The news did complicate life for my superiors. My boss, Vice Admiral Biggs, tried to contact Admiral Felix Stump, commander-in-chief of the Pacific Fleet, presumably to discuss President Eisenhower's threat about what would happen if reports of the hydrogen bomb test leaked out. Admiral Biggs was told that Admiral Stump was working on the "*Patapsco* thing." Biggs took this to mean that Stump was physically aboard the *Patapsco*. He ordered his driver to take him and an aide to the ship, where I met him.

"Where is Admiral Stump?" Biggs demanded. I had to explain that Admiral Stump was not in the vicinity. Admiral Biggs left us frustrated and a bit embarrassed. But the press release breach must have been resolved. I heard no more about it.

★　★　★

My crew and I were supposed to have complete physical and dental exams every six months over a period of five years. After the first half-dozen exams, no negative results surfaced. The rest of the exams were canceled, and we relegated the experience to history. As far as I know, I suffered no ill effects from our exposure to the Castle Bravo fallout.

Others were less fortunate. A Japanese fishing boat, the *Lucky Dragon Five*, was seventy-five miles east of Bikini when the bomb exploded. They were covered with a white powder—pulverized, radioactive coral. When the boat reached Japan two weeks later, the crew showed signs of radiation sickness: headaches, bleeding gums, blisters, and hair falling out. The boat's radio operator died from exposure seven months later.

Two days after the explosion, US officials evacuated the more than three hundred residents of Rongelap Atoll, which lay about 125 miles east of Ground Zero. They, too, suffered from symptoms of radiation exposure. Scientists later estimated they'd received 175 roentgens in just a few hours.

The original residents of Bikini Atoll were unaffected by the Castle Bravo bomb, but they never were returned to their contaminated former home.

Today, the general public is for the most part unaware and uninterested in the power and dangers of the H-bomb. Yet we need to be aware. Our enemies will continue to develop and refine weapons, and it's important that we stay ahead of them. During the Iraq war that began in 2003, President George W. Bush suggested that, while we have been opposed to preemptive military action throughout our country's history, given a new era of global terror, such preemptive action may need to become the new normal. This "Bush Doctrine" is reminiscent of humorist Artemus Ward's counsel on readiness: "Thrice armed is he that hath his quarrel just; and four times he who gets his fist in fust."

I certainly hope that no rogue nation, tyrannical dictator, or terrorist organization will threaten our existence and way of life to the point where preemptive strikes are necessary. But the security of our nation and of the world is fragile, and we must remain vigilant and prepared to do what must be done.

Still, Castle Bravo is just one example of how easy it is to underestimate the terrible power we now hold in our hands. Weapons of mass destruction are monstrous. There are nearly 16,000 nuclear weapons spread among nine nations. Surely, given the destructive force of a nuclear explosion, one such weapon is more than enough. Accidents and miscalculations can have tragic, catastrophic results. Good progress has been made by the nations in outlawing some of these weapons. But we should use all means necessary to rid the world of the rest.

Doing so draws a dividing line between those who would preserve civilization and those who in their lust for power would destroy civilization. Ridding the world of nuclear weapons may be accomplished by sanctioning, isolating, or depriving rogue states of needed resources. Or it may require military action. In any case, our vigilance and forcefulness must be matched, at all times, by wisdom—a consciousness of the weight of our decisions. As a veteran of the war that brought such weapons into existence, and a survivor of Castle Bravo, I believe all of us involved wish we had better protected the world of nations from this curse.

★ 13 ★
ENDINGS AND BEGINNINGS

IN DECEMBER 1954, my family and I enjoyed our third Christmas together in Honolulu. The shipping industry was on strike, but it allowed through a ship carrying Christmas trees for the military. So Morena, the kids, and I celebrated at home in the traditional manner. It was to be our last Christmas on the islands. A few days later, I received orders to report to the Fleet Antiaircraft Training Center at Dam Neck, Virginia. I was to be an instructor and range officer in the gunnery department. My days as captain of the *Patapsco* were ending.

It was the end for the *Patapsco* as well. On the day I was to transfer command to an ambitious naval reserve officer named Howard Wellsman, we received a dispatch ordering the ship to proceed to Astoria, Oregon, for decommissioning after fourteen years of gallantry. Poor Howard's duty was to return the *Patapsco* to the mainland so it could be relegated to the scrap heap.

(The *Patapsco* would ultimately be sold to a fishing company for $2 million. The cargo fuel tanks were converted to refrigerator storage for fish. She's now known as the *SS Patapsco*.)

Though I was sorry to see my first command come to a close, it was also a relief. A captain's responsibilities are tremendous. I was ready to take on shore duties for a couple of years, which I anticipated would be followed by another command.

At Dam Neck, my job did not require actual classroom instruction. We had guns of every caliber mounted along the beach that navy students could fire out over the ocean. My task was to train gun crews to maintain, repair, and fire every type of antiaircraft gun then installed on our navy ships. I worked in a hundred-foot-high control tower from which I could communicate with people at the gun mounts. I could have taken advantage of the supply of cotton available for plugging one's ears, but I felt it was too restrictive to use it. Two years later, a doctor told me I had damaged my hearing.

We lived in a house in Oceana, which was about five miles from Virginia Beach and twelve miles from Dam Neck. It was the closest Morena had ever come to having a dream home: four bedrooms, a fireplace, a detached garage, and a big yard with huge trees, a garden, a barbecue pit, and a pony stable. The purchase price was $14,500.

It was a pleasure to get reacquainted with friends from our old church in Norfolk. Morena took on an unexpected new ministry when she was invited to hold Bible classes for the entire student body of a Christian school for black students in Virginia Beach. This was at a time when black and white children were still segregated. Later, at a school banquet in her honor, Morena was the only white person present.

Throughout my navy career, I had worked with fellow Navigators and tried to serve the Navigator mission of spreading the gospel message and training others to do the same. I had also stayed in touch with the head Navigator, Dawson Trotman. In the spring of 1956, Dawson had joined with Billy Graham to conduct a spiritual campaign in Richmond, Virginia. The Trotmans invited Morena and me, as well as my old shipmate Lester Spencer and his wife, Martha, to join them and stay at the same hotel. Soon after we arrived, Dawson cornered me in the hotel lobby. He wanted me to leave the navy and join the Navigator staff.

I was less than enthusiastic about his proposal. I was at the height of my career. I'd been selected for promotion to lieutenant commander and was scheduled to be given command of another ship soon. I reminded Dawson that twenty years ago we'd had a similar conversation and agreed that the best way I could further the Navigator ministry was to make a career of the navy. I told him about my fruitful ministry.

As always, Dawson was quick on the trigger. He quoted John 15:2: "Every branch that beareth fruit, he purgeth it, that it may bring forth more fruit." He had no doubt that I should be pruned from the navy.

Three years before, Dawson had come to visit me and my family in Honolulu. He told me then that he had made his contribution to The Navigators. Trained men were in place and ready to take over just as soon as he got out of the way. He said he was a "bottleneck" to growth and expansion. I didn't take his comments too seriously at the time, and I doubt either of us was thinking about them that day in Virginia.

After an evangelistic meeting that evening, Dawson set up a late dinner for Morena and me, the Spencers, and some of the staff from the Navigator and Billy Graham organizations. There I met Dawson's right-hand man, thirty-five-year-old Lorne Sanny, who would become an important figure in my life. At the close of dinner, Dawson asked those present to pray that I would soon leave the navy, and that Morena and I would join the Navigator staff in Colorado.

Morena and I left Richmond and returned to our happy home and career in Oceana without giving Dawson an answer. At the time, I was not very open to his plan. But soon after, my health took a bad turn. I began finding it difficult to climb to the top of the control tower or perform difficult physical tasks. I simply ran out of breath. The Dam Neck navy doctor thought my situation was serious enough to recommend having me discharged from the navy due to physical disability. He started the administrative wheels in motion.

My condition deteriorated so much that I was hospitalized. The days turned into weeks. Finally, Morena had seen enough. She felt that the Lord was speaking clearly. "Jim," she said, "you are not ever going to get out of the hospital until you accept Dawson's invitation."

I took her advice seriously. If I had learned anything during my career in the military, it was the value of obedience, sacrifice, and service. They were the foundations that every branch of the service stands on. Nothing of significance could be accomplished without them. Moreover, these values were the way we demonstrated love to God and each other. Perhaps the time had come to obey a new calling, sacrifice my future in the navy, and serve the Lord full-time.

After thinking and praying on it, I decided I would accept retirement and leave the navy after twenty-four years.

Almost immediately, my health began to improve. After a fifty-five-day stay, I was discharged from the hospital, and I resumed normal exercise and work. Only months later did I discover that the cause of my trouble was an allergic reaction to sulfur fumes escaping from Virginia's industrial plants.

A survey board convened and, based on my previous condition, recommended my retirement. I did not fight the decision.

During the second week of June, Lila Trotman and some girls traveling with her stopped in Oceana for an evening visit. They were en route to Schroon Lake, New York, for a week-long conference. Dawson was to be the main speaker. I had said nothing to the Trotmans of my recent decision to accept Dawson's offer. I did not realize until later that Lila was on a spy mission to observe us and see if we were in good spiritual health. If we were, why wouldn't we respond to Dawson's invitation?

I asked Lila to tell Dawson I would come up to Schroon Lake on Tuesday, June 19, to talk with him. I didn't tell her why. My plan was to inform Dawson in person that we had decided the Lord wanted us to accept his invitation to work full-time with The Navigators.

I arranged to take a week's leave from my duties at Dam Neck. I would leave Monday afternoon with Ross Baldwin, director of the Portsmouth Servicemen's Center, drive all night, and arrive at Schroon Lake on Tuesday morning.

Lila traveled on ahead of us. On Sunday at Schroon Lake, she and Dawson sat down for a serious conversation. She said she'd had a strong premonition that Dawson's life would end and that his death would be associated with water. Dawson had no such premonition, but for much of the afternoon he answered Lila's questions and gave her messages for various friends and staff members. At the time, I knew nothing about their discussion.

Ross and I left Virginia on Monday as planned, drove all night, and arrived at Schroon Lake at 6:30 Tuesday morning. A heavy pall silenced the camp. No one stirred. I spotted a conferee having a quiet time and interrupted him. "Is this a Navigator conference? If it is, it's the deadest Navigator conference I've ever seen."

Soberly, he replied, "It may have something to do with the accident yesterday."

"What accident?"

"A man drowned."

"Who was it?"

"I don't recall his name, but he seemed to be in charge around here."

"Was it Dawson Trotman?" I asked.

"Yes. *That* was his name. How did you know?"

I couldn't believe it. Dawson Trotman, the man who had mentored me spiritually for years and helped link me with Morena— gone? It made no sense. Dawson was only fifty years old.

"Excuse me," I said to Ross. "I have to walk this off."

Unfamiliar with the camp, I ended my walk at the water-front. About the time I got there, my deeply grieved friend Jack Wyrtzen arrived in his speedboat. He invited me to breakfast so he could tell me about the events of the previous day.

Jack, whose Word of Life ministry owned the conference center at Schroon Lake, spent his summers on the property. During a conference break on Monday afternoon, he'd invited Dawson to take a ride with him in his speedboat. When they got to the dock, several conferees were relaxing there. Dawson, always generous and wanting to serve, invited some of them along for the ride. One man, Norman Larsen, got in the front seat with Jack. Three girls got in the rear seat. Dawson and two other girls perched on the back of the rear seat with their feet behind the three seated girls.

Always cautious, Dawson inquired if there was anyone in the boat who couldn't swim. One of the girls, Allene Beck, could not. Dawson locked arms with Allene on his left and the other girl on his right.

With eight people in what was supposed to be a five-passenger boat, they sped out onto the lake. A little more than a mile from land, Jack turned his head toward Dawson. Above the noise of the motor, he shouted, "Isn't this fun? Let's go get Lila." Dawson nodded. Jack applied full rudder to turn the boat around.

The water was rough, with moderate waves. As the boat began a sharp turn, it slapped into a wave with such force that from their high center of gravity, Dawson and the girl on his left, Allene, were thrown overboard.

Dawson was a good swimmer, but he knew Allene couldn't

swim, so he began treading water while holding her up to the surface. Jack threw some lifejackets into the water and circled the boat back to Dawson and Allene. Those on board pulled Allene from his arms.

The instant she was freed, Dawson's arms drifted apart, and he began to sink.

One of the girls in the boat was a skilled swimmer and experienced lifeguard. She dove overboard and got under Dawson to bring him to the surface. Then, for the first time in her life, she developed severe leg and stomach cramps. To save her own life, she had to let go of him.

Lila had gone into the town to purchase groceries. On the drive back to camp, she suddenly felt such a heavy heart that she pulled over to the side of the road to pray about her premonition. Her main prayer was that when the time came, the Lord would give her the strength to be a good example to others.

Back at camp, a friend ran to tell Lila what had happened. She arrived at the Trotmans' cabin at the same time Lila did. "Dawson has fallen overboard," the friend said, "and they haven't found him yet."

Amazingly, Lila's immediate reaction was, "I know."

Lila stayed at Schroon Lake for the entire week of the conference. Because she and I were old friends, I spent time with her daily. Among other things, I learned that the moment she pulled off the road to pray was the exact moment Dawson fell overboard.

Three days after the drowning, Morena opened our mailbox in Oceana and found a note from Dawson. He'd become fond of our twins, Don and David, during his stay with us in

Honolulu three years earlier. After hearing an update on them from Lila on Sunday, he'd put a pair of one-dollar bills into an envelope and mailed them along with a note saying we should buy some "junk," meaning candy, for the twins. At the time, Dawson and Lila's weekly pay from The Navigators was only twenty-two dollars a week.

At first, Dawson's death was a puzzle to me. Then I reflected on our conversation during that Honolulu visit about The Navigators being ready to take off when Dawson got out of the way. Perhaps God was so determined that The Navigators' ministry increase and multiply that he did not intervene in the natural events on the lake. He changed leadership according to his schedule.

Lorne Sanny arrived at Schroon Lake on Wednesday of that week. He told me about his future plans: "I have known for some time I would eventually inherit the responsibility of The Navigators. I have already decided that instead of a one-man operation, it will be a team operation. The Lord has given me the names of the men he wants to help me. You are one of them."

This was only the second time I had met Lorne, and I didn't realize how many of Dawson's characteristics he had picked up. One of them was that if he liked you, he wanted you nearby. "I am aware of the negotiations Dawson has been having with you," he told me, "and I am going to double those efforts. How soon can you get out of the navy and move to Colorado?"

I wanted to make sure there were a real need and a real job for me with The Navigators. It wasn't clear in Lorne's mind as to all I would do. He put my job description in terms of a baseball utility fielder—a player who filled the most urgent need. But one duty was already determined: I would take over management of Glen Eyrie, the eight-hundred-acre estate that served as Navigator headquarters.

The more I thought about Lorne's team concept and my potential role as a utility player, the more I felt that the Lord was calling me to The Navigators. The decision to move was not easy for Morena. She loved our home, our church, and the schools our children attended. But in the end she willingly traded the trees around our Virginia home for the mountains of Colorado.

I filled out reams of paperwork to make my retirement from the navy official. At the stroke of midnight on October 31, 1956, a burden rolled off my shoulders. For the first time in twenty-four years, I didn't have to be anywhere at any precise time. No one was checking up on me. I'd enjoyed a rewarding career, serving through two hot wars and one cold one, but I thought the navy would probably get along without me. Once the transition was complete, I never looked back. It was time for a new challenge.

For the next twenty-seven years, I devoted my full-time energies to serving the Lord through the ministry of The Navigators. I found that my navy career had prepared me well for working with and leading people, and for fighting battles on a spiritual plane instead of the high seas. It was probably the most rewarding time of a life filled with adventures and unexpected blessings.

I will forever be grateful for all of it.

EPILOGUE

DAWSON TROTMAN ONCE SAID I was the only man he knew who could disagree with him and still be blessed by God. I don't know about that, but the blessings that I experienced so often in my life did not end when I retired from the navy. Since our daughter Marobeth was followed by five boys, Morena and I were thrilled that our seventh and last child was another daughter. Joy was born December 6, 1960, in Colorado Springs. Being a husband to Morena and father to my children has been one of the great privileges of my life.

The opportunity to serve the Lord through the ministry of The Navigators at Glen Eyrie and around the world has been another great privilege. I remained a utility player during my twenty-two years on the full-time staff in Colorado, including stints as deputy president and chair of the board of directors. I also wrote two books prior to this one, *Meditation* and *Living Legacy*. Under Lorne Sanny's wise guidance, The Navigators expanded exponentially and established their mission for future generations: evangelizing, establishing, and equipping.

In 1978, when Joy entered college and all of our kids were out of the house, Morena and I moved to London. For the next three years, I provided leadership for The Navigators in nations throughout Europe, the Middle East, and Africa. In 1981, we moved to Washington, D.C., to conduct a ministry among government personnel. I did a regular Bible study in the White House with President Ronald Reagan's legislative assistant. Though he never asked anyone to hold calls, it was always unusually quiet during our meetings. He said that the minute I left, the calls started up again.

I officially retired from The Navigators in 1983, but I continue to represent the ministry at events around the world. I am still known as "Navigator Number Six."

I have never forgotten my navy roots. I often attend and speak at veterans events, and periodically I fly back to Pearl Harbor for the annual events that commemorate the 1941 attack. I consider myself a patriot. These visits are a chance to honor my country, the friends and fellow servicemen who gave their lives defending it, and the friends still here who can recall those times with me. Wherever I go, I spread the message I've already mentioned in this book: Freedom is worth protecting. Weakness invites aggression. Remember Pearl Harbor. Keep America strong.

On that long-ago Sunday morning, I witnessed shocking

treachery, devastation, and death. I will never forget it. But there is another side to infamy, one I have known since the moment I said a prayer in a turret on April 8, 1935—the joy and peace I find in Jesus Christ. The Bible tells us that the Lord is more than a match for any problem we face: "God is our refuge and strength, a very present help in trouble." I truly understood this for the first time at Pearl Harbor, when I thought the *Neosho* was about to explode. Once I put the matter in God's hands, my worries ceased and were replaced by an amazing sense of peace. "I'll see you in a minute," I told God. God saw fit to put off the time when I would see him face to face.

What I've learned from that experience and others since is that God does not respond to false alarms. If I feel he's not paying attention, it's because I'm not in any real trouble. And if I *am* in real trouble, I don't have to worry about it. I know he's there. He may not handle things the way I would prefer, but I recognize he's got things under control.

This discovery influenced the rest of my life. I simply don't worry much. It is likely the secret to my longevity and how I maintained an even keel through so many years at war. I've had the blood pressure of a teenager for most of my days.

I do miss my wife. Morena passed away in 2010. We had been married for sixty-eight years. The hardest part comes in the evening, in not being able to share what's happened that day with her. She is one of the many blessings I did not deserve but was granted anyway.

Another blessing is the opportunities the Lord continues to provide. Even though I am 103 years old, I travel frequently and speak at several events each month. My mission now is to continue to share the Good News of Jesus Christ. I'm told that through television, radio, and personal appearances, as well as print-media interviews, my message reached more than ten million people in 2015 alone. Some of these connections have defied explanation. The only answer is that God wanted them to occur.

The truth is that these last few years have been the best of my life. I have so much fun that I don't look back at yesterday or forward to tomorrow. I live one day at a time.

APPENDIX

HONORING JIM DOWNING

Congressional Record

113th Congress (2013-2014)

HON. DOUG LAMBORN

OF COLORADO
IN THE HOUSE OF REPRESENTATIVES
WEDNESDAY, JULY 31, 2012
(Extensions of Remarks—July 31, 2013)

Mr. LAMBORN. Mr. Speaker, I rise today in honor of Jim Downing who will be celebrating his 100th birthday on August 22, 2013. Throughout his century of life, he loyally served the United States Navy, was a devoted husband and father and faithful to his Creator.

He enlisted in the Navy in 1932, and was assigned to the USS *West Virginia* where he held a variety of roles onboard. On April 8, 1935 Jim gave his life to the Lord and vowed to follow Him wherever he was led. Jim was involved with original founders of The Navigators who discipled him and gave him the tools to evangelize to his whole ship and lead regular Bible studies onboard.

A survivor of the attack on Pearl Harbor, he helped rescue men from his ship and fight fires onboard. He later rose to the rank of Lieutenant, commanding his own ship the USS *Patapsco*. While at sea in 1954 his ship was showered with the radio-active ash from the "H" bomb being tested at Bikini Atoll. He served as an advisor to the Brazilian Fleet in Rio de Janeiro and later became an assistant professor of Naval Science at the Merchant Marine Academy.

Jim retired in 1956 with 24 years of service in the Navy and went to work for The Navigators for the next 22 years. During the years he served on The Navigator staff he held many capacities including, Divisional Director for Europe the Middle East and Africa with Headquarters in London, Vice President, Deputy to President Lorne Sarmy [Sanny], and Chairman of the Board of Directors.

Jim and his wife Morena were married for 68 years before her passing. He has authored two books, *Meditation* and *Living Legacy*, both of which have been very well received. He has spent over 78 years working for the Lord and being a disciple maker wherever he is located. While he retired from full-time ministry in 1983, he has not retired from teaching others about the

Lord and is on the volunteer staff of The Navigators' Collegiate Ministry.

To this day, Jim is investing in the lives of thousands of young people through personal discipleship and The Navigator's Collegiate and Military Ministry. I am greatly honored to help celebrate 100 years of life for a man who has been influential to so many communities around the world through his service and devotion to the Lord.

NOTES

If not otherwise noted, the material for this book comes from my personal memories, diaries, ship's logs, my book *Living Legacy*, and previous writings for family and friends. I have reconstructed conversations to the best of my recollection.

PROLOGUE

viii   *Honolulu, December 6*: Walter Lord, *Day of Infamy* (New York: Henry Holt and Company, 1957), 1, 7.

CHAPTER 1: DREAMS AND SHADOWS

3   *Proposed Germany-Mexico alliance, declaration of war*: Erik Larson, *Dead Wake* (New York: Crown Publishers, 2015), 337–343.

13   *Sarnoff prediction*: "More About Sarnoff, Part One," American Experience, Public Broadcasting Service, accessed March 10, 2016, http://www.pbs.org /wgbh/amex/technology/bigdream/masarnoff.html.

16   *Stock market losses*: "Dow Jones Industrial Average All-Time Largest One Day Gains and Losses," *Wall Street Journal*, accessed March 10, 2016, http:// online.wsj.com/mdc/public/page/2_3047-djia_alltime.html.

CHAPTER 2: THE REAL WORLD

17   *Unemployment statistics*: "Timeline of the Great Depression," Hyper History, accessed March 10, 2016, at http://www.hyperhistory.com/online_n2 /connections_n2/great_depression.html.

28   *Long Beach earthquake*: Molly Hennessy-Fiske, "1933 Long Beach Temblor Defined Southern California as 'Earthquake Country,'" *Los Angeles Times*, March 10, 2008, www.latimes.com/local/la-me-lbquake10mar10-story.html.

CHAPTER 4: INSIDE MAN

50 *Law for the Protection of German Blood and German Honor*: Daniel James Brown, *The Boys in the Boat* (New York: Penguin Books, 2013), 216.

51 *Hitler's tensest hours, Goebbels's summary*: Brown, *Boys in the Boat*, 252.

51 *Taxi drivers and garbage collectors*: Brown, *Boys in the Boat*, 298–99.

52 *"the Negro Owens"*: "The Triumph of Hitler," The History Place, accessed March 10, 2016, http://www.historyplace.com/worldwar2/triumph/tr-olympics.htm.

52 *Hitler on Christianity*: Albert Speer, *Inside the Third Reich* (New York: Simon and Schuster, 1970), 96.

53 *Japanese religion, government propaganda*: John W. Dower, *Cultures of War* (New York: W. W. Norton & Company, 2011), 295.

53 *Japan's imperial destiny*: Laura Hillenbrand, *Unbroken* (New York: Random House, 2010), 45–46.

CHAPTER 5: THEN THERE WAS MORENA

71 *"the way of a man with a maid"*: Proverbs 30:19.

71 *Morena's love diagnosis*: Song of Songs 2:5.

CHAPTER 6: FURY ON OAHU

75 *Fuchida's approach to Pearl Harbor, thoughts on morning*: Douglas T. Shinsato and Tadanori Urabe, *For That One Day: The Memoirs of Mitsuo Fuchida* (Kamuela, HI: eXperience, 2011), 85–90.

77 *Army radar station*: Gordon W. Prange, *At Dawn We Slept: The Untold Story of Pearl Harbor* (New York: Penguin Books, 1981), 500–501; Walter Lord, *Day of Infamy* (New York: Henry Holt and Company, 1957), 41–45.

78 *Japanese submarines and destroyer* Ward: Prange, *At Dawn We Slept*, 484–85, 495–98; Lord, *Day of Infamy*, 27–29, 58–62.

79 *Marshall's warning*: Prange, *At Dawn We Slept*, 494–95; Lord, *Day of Infamy*, 166–67.

80 *Fuchida signals attack force, Japanese fleet*: Prange, *At Dawn We Slept*, 502–504.

88 *Fuchida's bridge conversations with Nagumo, Kusaka*: Prange, *At Dawn We Slept*, 542–546; Shinsato and Urabe, *For That One Day*, 103–105.

CHAPTER 7: A DIFFERENT WORLD

94 *Island defenses*: Walter Lord, *Day of Infamy* (New York: Henry Holt and Company, 1957), 181–182.

94 *Kimmel throws away Marshall's warning*: Lord, *Day of Infamy*, 167–168.

95 *People rally*: Lord, *Day of Infamy*, 183–184; Frank Marqua, "Seventy Years Ago, Teams from San Jose State and Willamette Were in Hawaii for Fun and Football. Then the Japanese Attacked Pearl Harbor," Santa Rosa *Press Democrat*, December 6, 2011, http://www.pressdemocrat.com/news/2300442-181/seventy-years-ago-teams-from?page=0.

 98 *December 8, America awoke*: Craig Shirley, *December 1941* (Nashville, TN: Thomas Nelson, 2011), 154, 178–179.

 99 *Roosevelt's "infamy" speech*: Shirley, *December 1941*, 165, 167–169.

103 *Pearl Harbor casualties, damage*: Lord, *Day of Infamy*, 212; Gordon W. Prange, *At Dawn We Slept* (New York: Penguin Books, 1981), 539.

CHAPTER 8: NO SACRIFICE TOO GREAT

109 *"Delaying actions" statement*: Craig Shirley, *December 1941* (Nashville, TN: Thomas Nelson, 2011), 442.

110 *Hitler's views on America*: Jon Meacham, *Franklin and Winston: An Intimate Portrait of an Epic Friendship* (New York: Random House, 2003), 134.

113 *Vic McAnney letter, "learning more and more"*: LaVerne E. Tift, *Valiant in Fight: A Book of Remembrance* (Fresno, CA: Valiant Publications, 1990), 114.

117 *Vic McAnney's death, letter and comments about the author*: Tift, *Valiant in Fight*, 113, 119–122.

117 *Jack Armstrong death, conversation with LaVerne Tift*: Tift, *Valiant in Fight*, 132–133, 136–138.

118 *"Fear thou not" verse*: Isaiah 41:10.

120 *"it was a day"*: Walter Lord, *Day of Infamy* (New York: Henry Holt and Company, 1957), 213.

CHAPTER 11: CAPTAIN DOWNING

158 *Fuchida's conversion to Christianity*: Douglas T. Shinsato and Tadanori Urabe, *For That One Day* (Kamuela, HI: eXperience, 2011), 237–50.

CHAPTER 12: CASTLE BRAVO

161 *Operation Crossroads, Able bomb*: Connie Goldsmith, *Bombs over Bikini* (Minneapolis, MN: Twenty-First Century Books, 2014), 19–23.

162 *"like the bomb"*: Louis Réard as quoted in Brett Westwood & Stephen Moss, *Natural Histories* (London: Hodder & Stoughton, 2015).

162 *Baker bomb*: Goldsmith, *Bombs over Bikini*, 29–32.

162 *Hiroshima, Nagasaki bomb yields*: "Hiroshima, Nagasaki, and Subsequent Weapons Testing," World Nuclear Association, accessed March 10, 2016, http:// www.world-nuclear.org/information-library/safety-and-security/radiation-and -health/hiroshima,-nagasaki,-and-subsequent-weapons-testin.aspx.

163 *Fission vs. fusion*: Goldsmith, *Bombs over Bikini*, 39–41.

168 *Castle Bravo bomb*: "World's Biggest Bomb," Secrets of the Dead, Public Broadcasting Service, originally aired May 17, 2011; Goldsmith, *Bombs Over Bikini*, 42–45.

169 *Halderman quote, weather conditions*: "World's Biggest Bomb."

172 *press release*: "92 Crewmen on Atom-Showered Navy Ship Safe," *Honolulu Advertiser*, March 24, 1954.

173 *Holifield quote*: William J. Waugh, "Hydrogen Explosion Spread Radioactive Ash on Navy Tanker, Crew," *Ludington Daily News*, March 25, 1954, 10.

174 Lucky Dragon Five: Goldsmith, *Bombs over Bikini*, 53.

175 *Nearly 16,000 nuclear weapons: "The Facts," International Campaign to Abolish Nuclear Weapons, accessed May 2, 2016, http://www.icanw.org/the-facts/nuclear -arsenals/.*

EPILOGUE

189 *"God is our refuge"*: Psalm 46:1.

ABOUT THE AUTHORS

 **JIM DOWNING**, age 103, is a twenty-four-year US Navy veteran. He fought fires on and survived the sinking of the USS *West Virginia* during Japan's attack on Pearl Harbor on December 7, 1941. He captained the USS *Patapsco* during the Cold War, performed a host of missions on several ships around the world, and twice served stints as a navy instructor. While racing away from Bikini Atoll on March 1, 1954, Jim and his crew were showered with radioactive ash from Castle Bravo, the most powerful nuclear bomb ever detonated by the United States and the largest US nuclear contamination accident.

But Jim Downing is more than a military man—he is also a man of deep faith. On April 8, 1935, in a West Virginia turret, he dedicated his life to God. He joined the ministry of Dawson Trotman, becoming "Navigator Number Six" and helping to spread the tenets of Christianity throughout the Pacific Fleet. He served full-time with The Navigators for twenty-seven years, including as deputy president and board chair, and continues to represent the ministry at events around the world. He is the author of the books *Meditation* and *Living Legacy: Reflections on Dawson Trotman and Lorne Sanny.*

Raised in Plevna, Missouri, Jim was married to Morena Holmes for sixty-eight years before her death in 2010. He is the father of seven children and lives in Colorado Springs, Colorado.

With the publication of *The Other Side of Infamy*, Jim was recognized by Guinness World Records as the oldest male author on record.

 **JAMES LUND** is an award-winning collaborator and editor, and the coauthor of *A Dangerous Faith* and *Danger Calling*. He works with bestselling authors and public figures such as George Foreman, Kathy Ireland, Max Lucado, Tim Brown, Randy Alcorn, and Jim Daly. Book sales from Jim's projects exceed three million copies. He lives with his wife, Angela, in Central Oregon. Visit his website at jameslundbooks.com.

MORE FROM
JIM DOWNING

ISBN 978-0-9729023-8-0

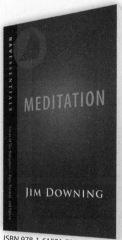

ISBN 978-1-61521-725-0

As one of the original Navigators, author Jim Downing's partnership with Dawson Trotman and Lorne Sanny has given him a perspective like no other. In *Living Legacy*, Jim shares personal reflections, leadership lessons, and humorous anecdotes of two men whose lives have influenced millions.

In this classic Navigator message, Jim Downing explores meditation, communion, and obedience. He gives practical instruction and encouragement to readers who want to experience a more abiding relationship with God.